Copyright © 2023 L. Sanders

All rights reserved. This publication is copyright. No part of this book may be reproduced, stored in a retrieval system or transmitted in any form or by any means, electronic, mechanical, photocopying, recording or otherwise, without the prior written permission of the copyright holder.

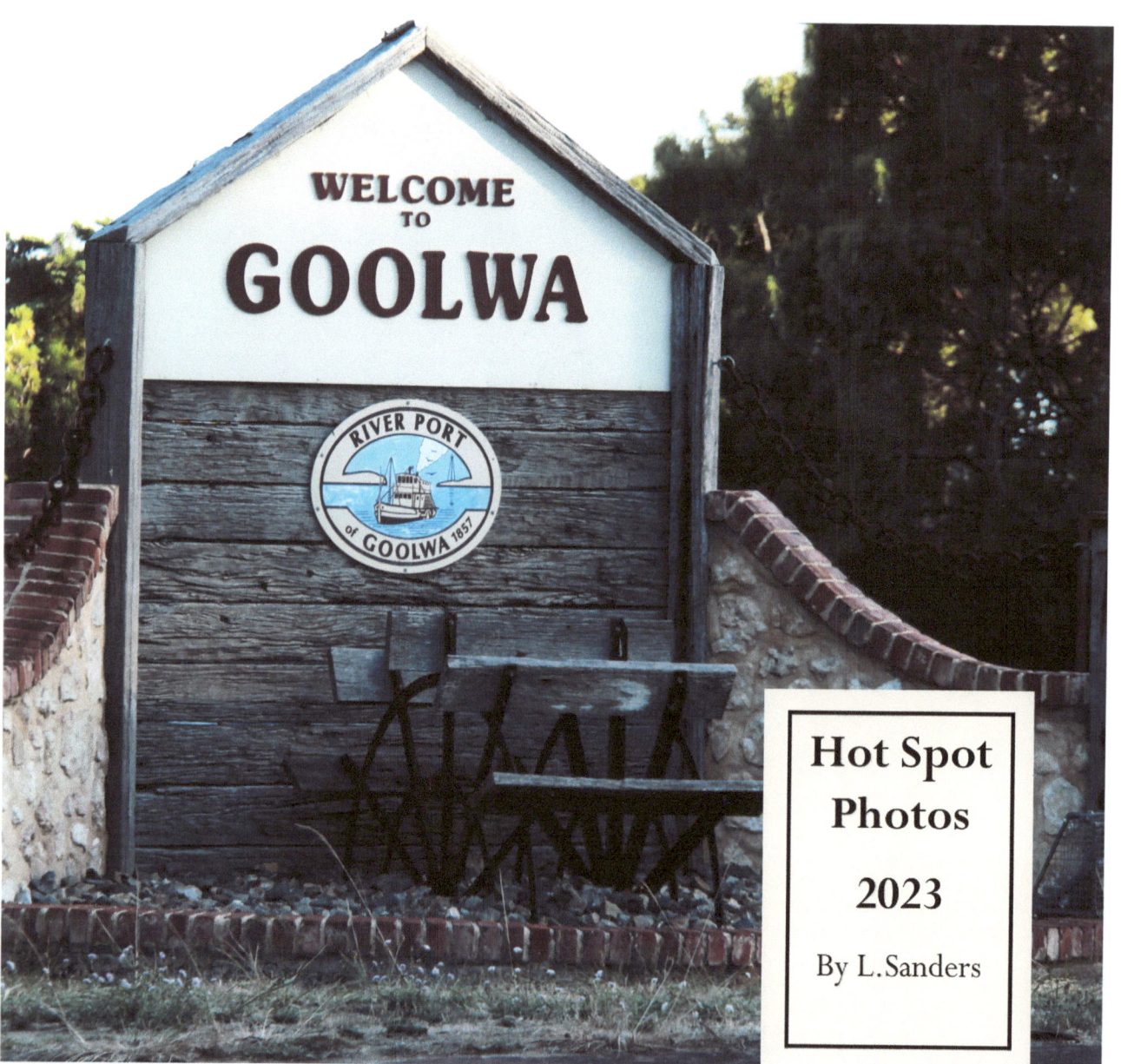

Hot Spot Photos

2023

By L.Sanders

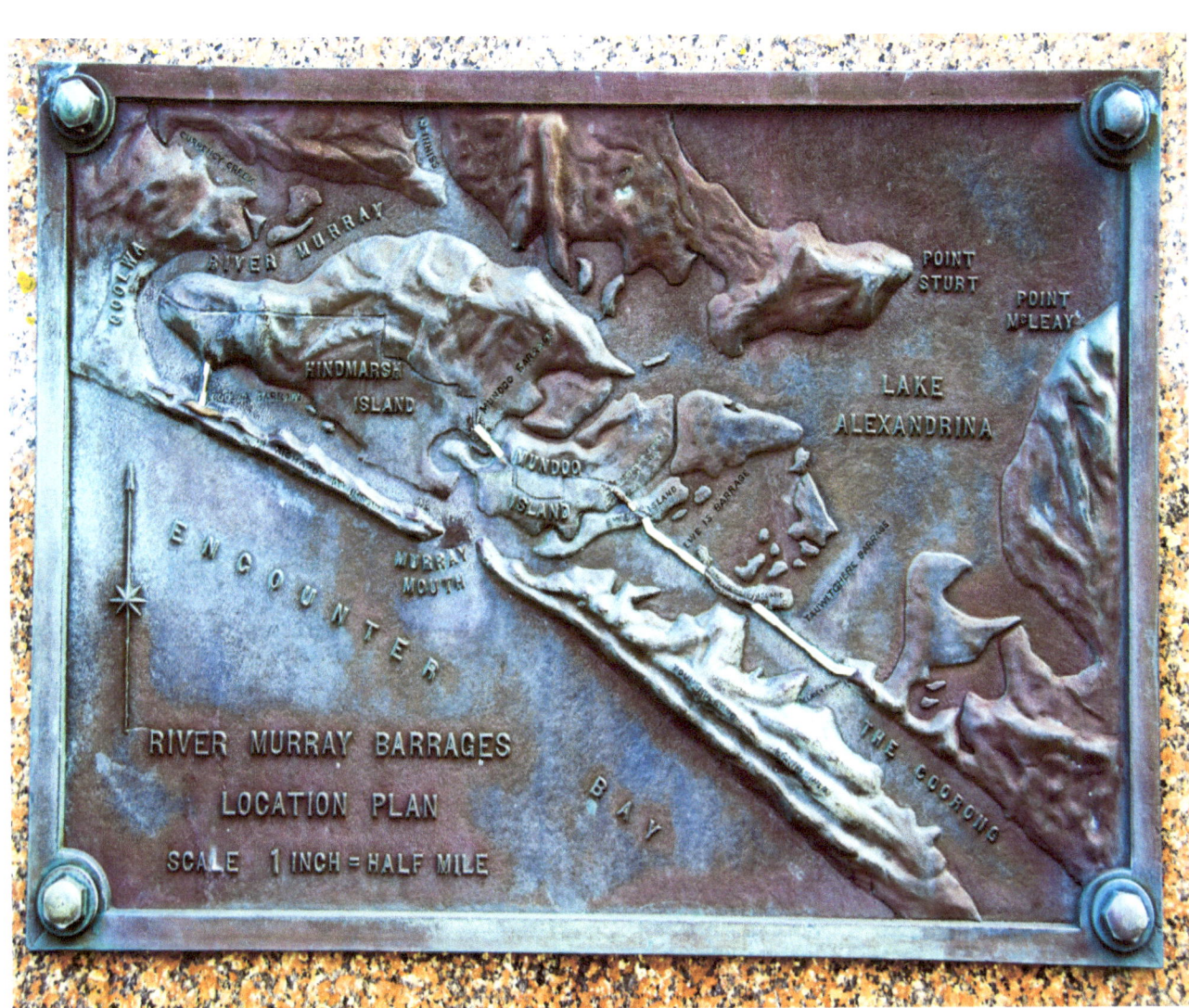

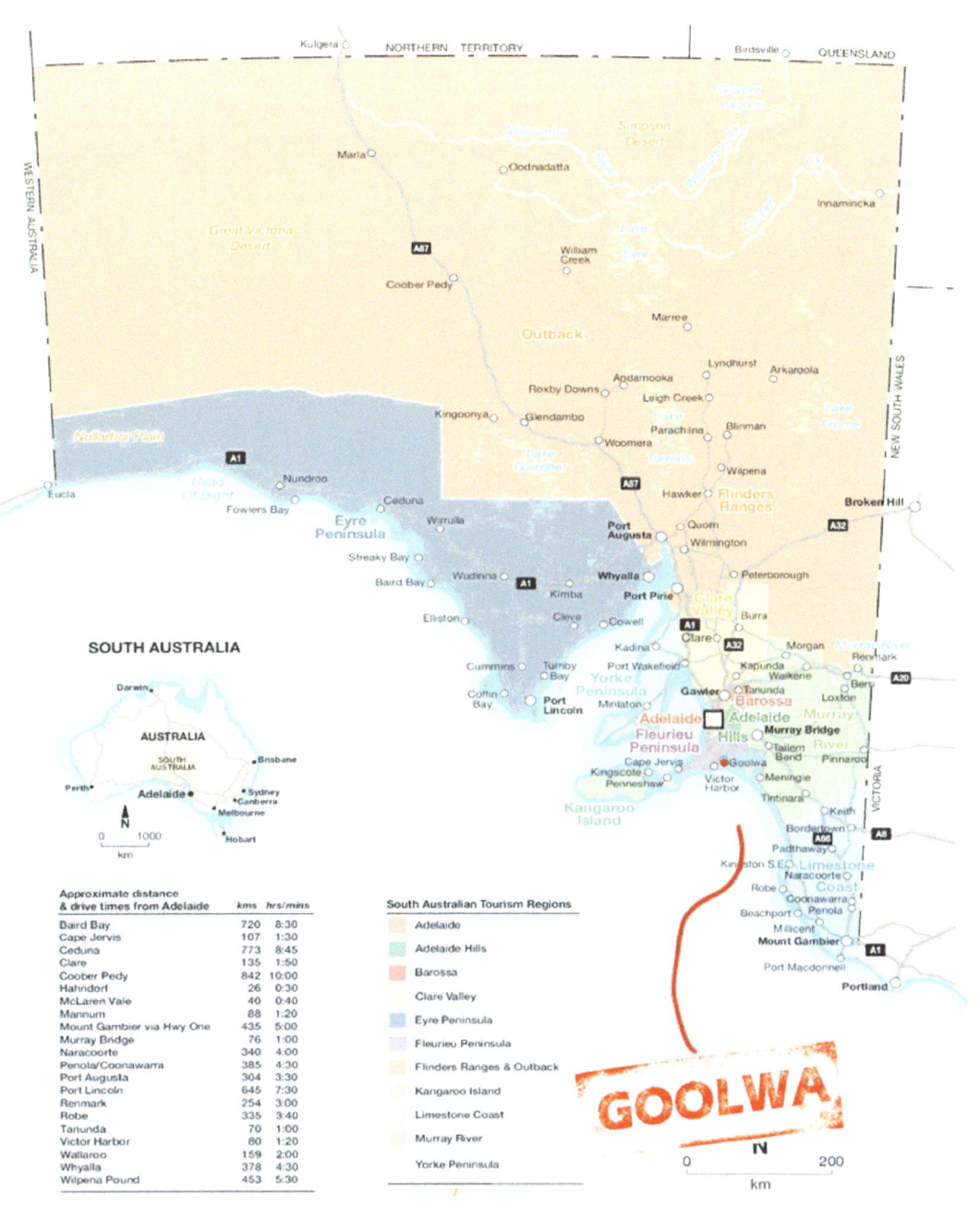

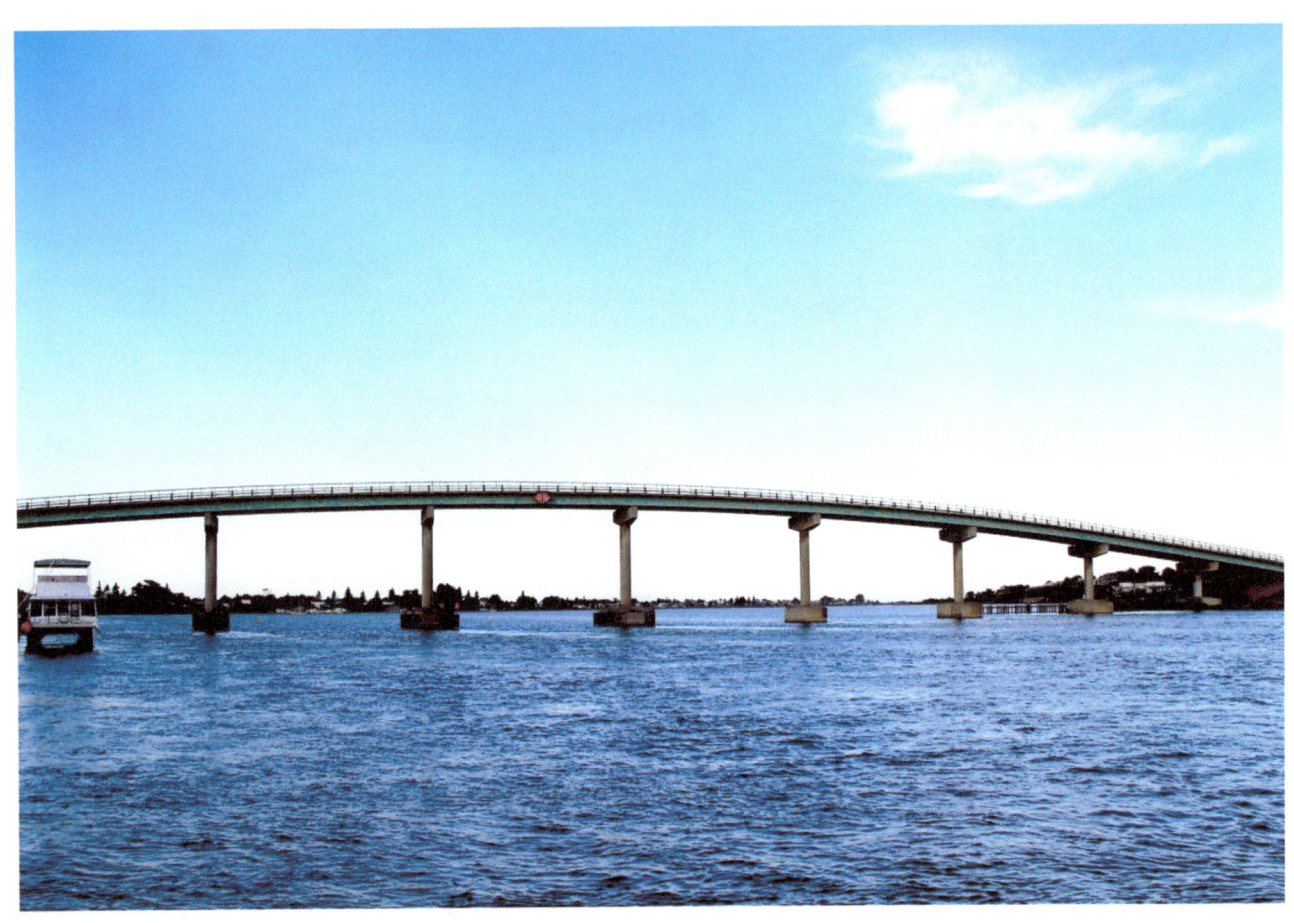

THE EXPANSE OF HINDMARSH ISLAND BRIDGE

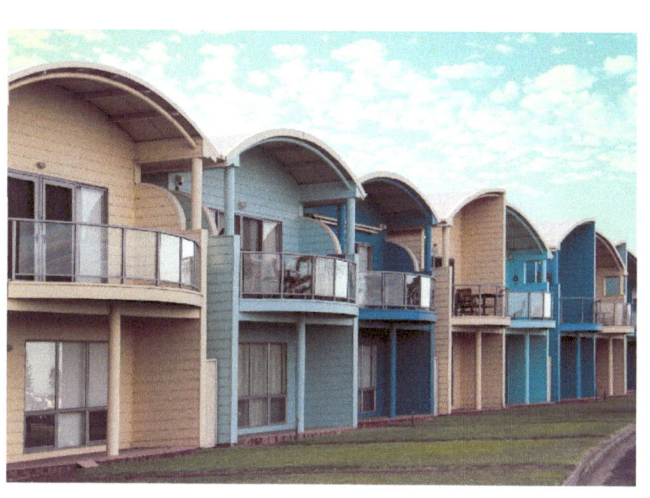 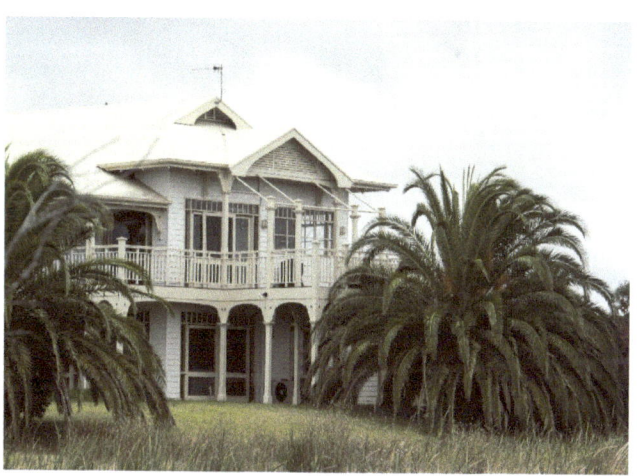

# Discovering the magic of Goolwa

A charming town nestled on the southern coast of Australia's Fleurieu Peninsula with its stunning landscape and diverse wildlife, Goolwa is a unique and captivating destination that offers a perfect blend of history, charm, and fascinating facts. The area is home to a myriad of ecosystems, from the Murray River to the Coorong National Park and the Southern Ocean, all supporting a wealth of plant and animal life. Explore sweeping sand dunes, vibrant wetlands, and lush eucalypt forests, all within reach.

Goolwa's rich history dates back to the 1800s, where it served as one of the main ports for paddle steamers on the river Murray, playing a vital role in the transport of goods across Australia. It was also the centre of South Australia's whaling industry, making it an important part of the state's history. Explore the town's historic buildings and landmarks, such as the wooden wharf and the Cockle Train, the first public railway with iron rails built in Australia.

Visitors can take a self-guided tour of the Goolwa Barrage, marvelling at the incredible engineering feats that have allowed the town to thrive. Foodies will love Goolwa's range of restaurants, cafes, and bakeries, serving up everything from fresh seafood to artisanal coffee and delightful baked goods.

Goolwa's unique blend of history, charm, and natural beauty is sure to enchant visitors. The town offers excellent photographic opportunities, and the chance to capture the essence of this captivating destination.

Come and discover the magic of Goolwa for yourself.

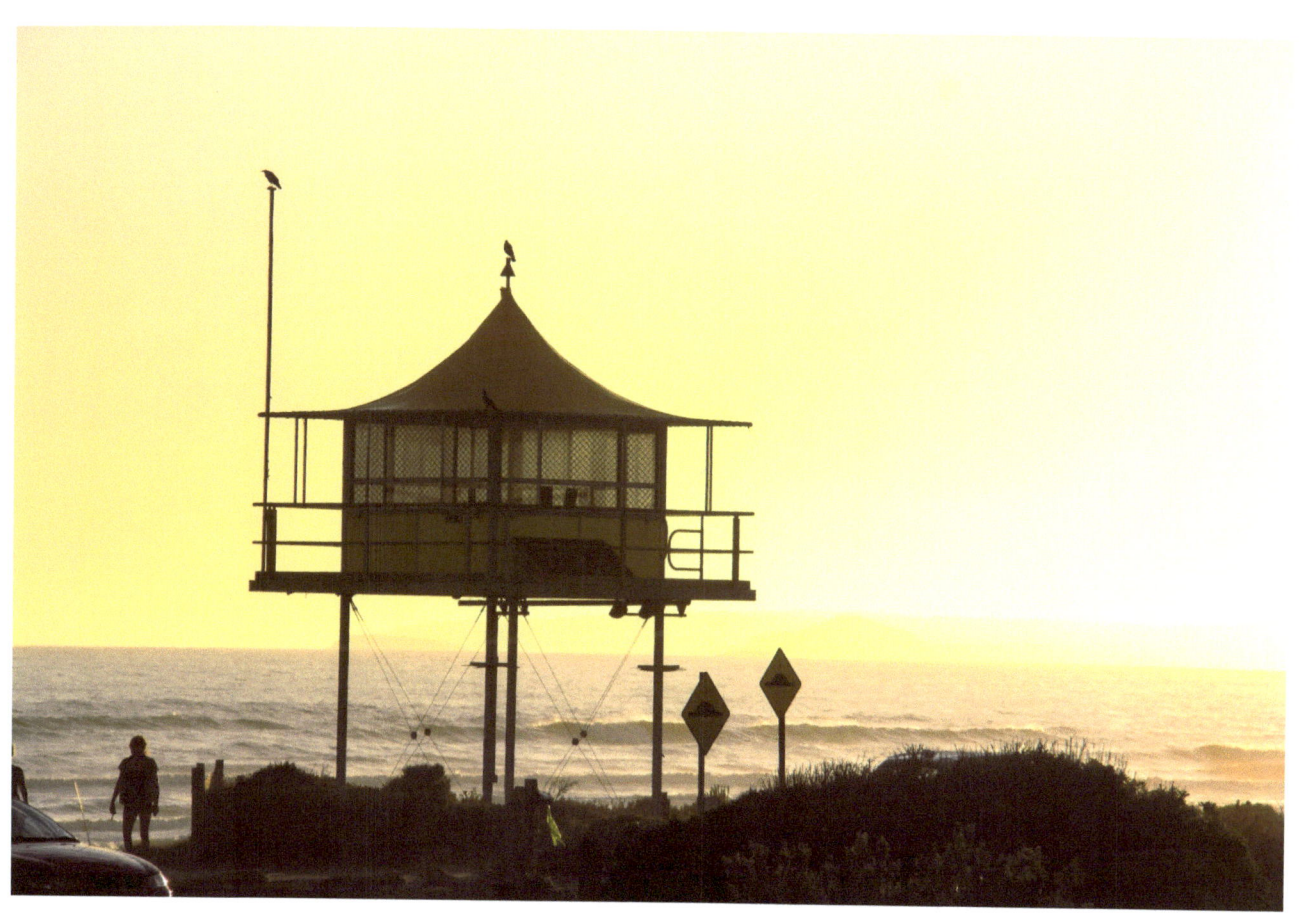

*SURF LIVESAVING RESCUE OBSERVATION HUT*

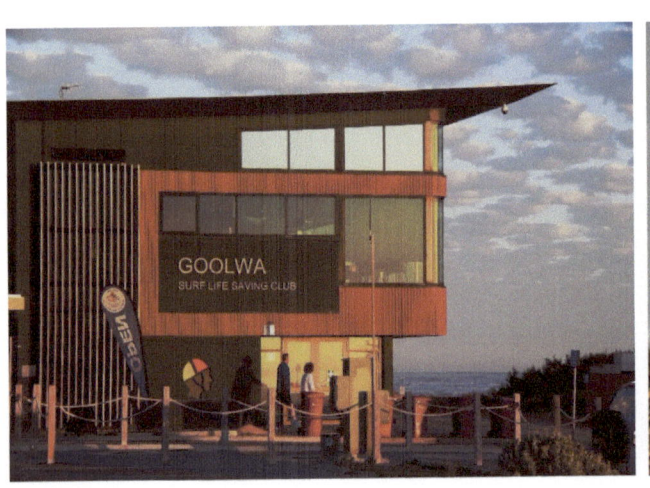 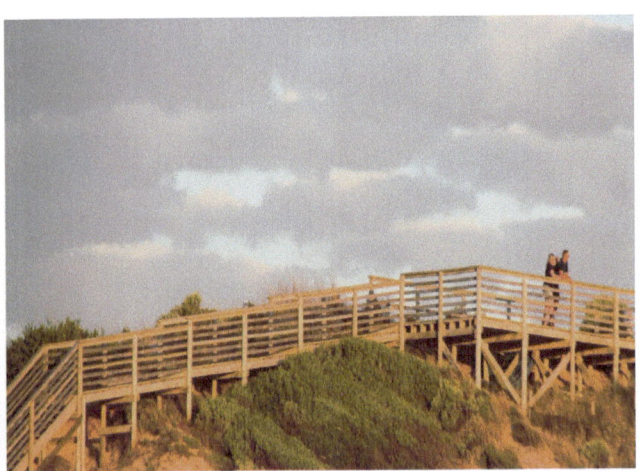

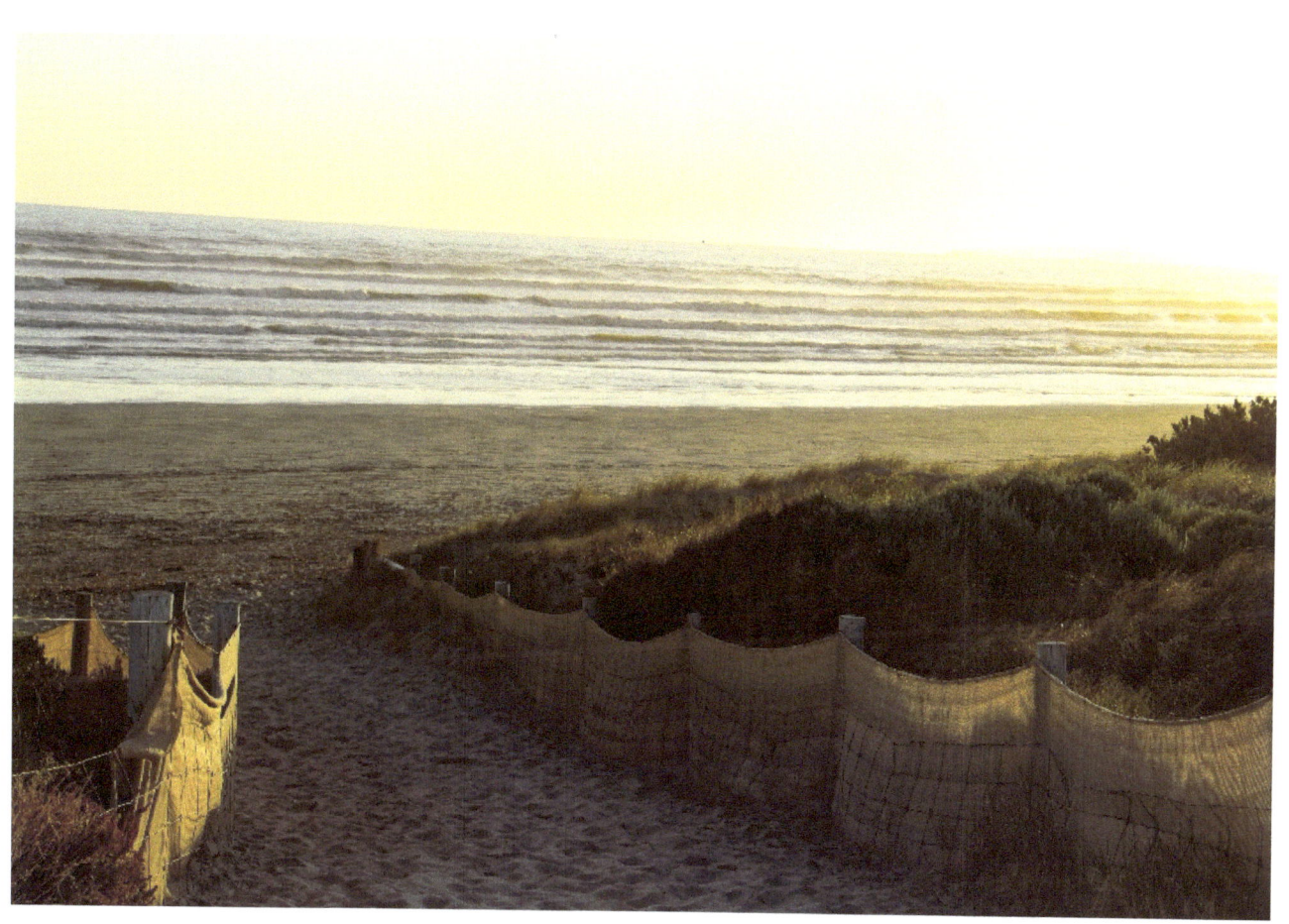

*SANDY ENTRANCE TO BEACH*

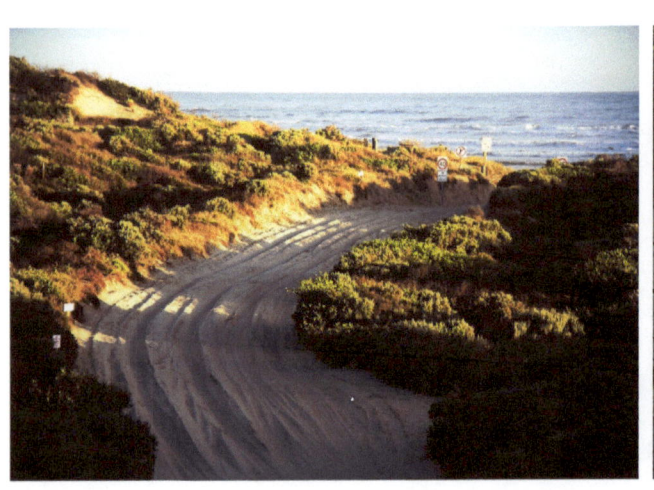 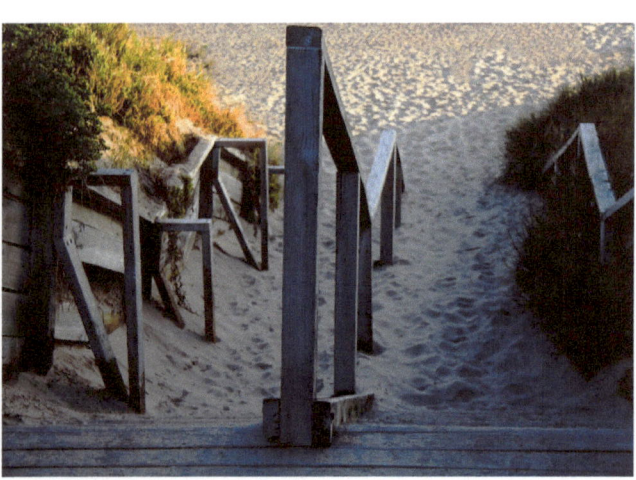

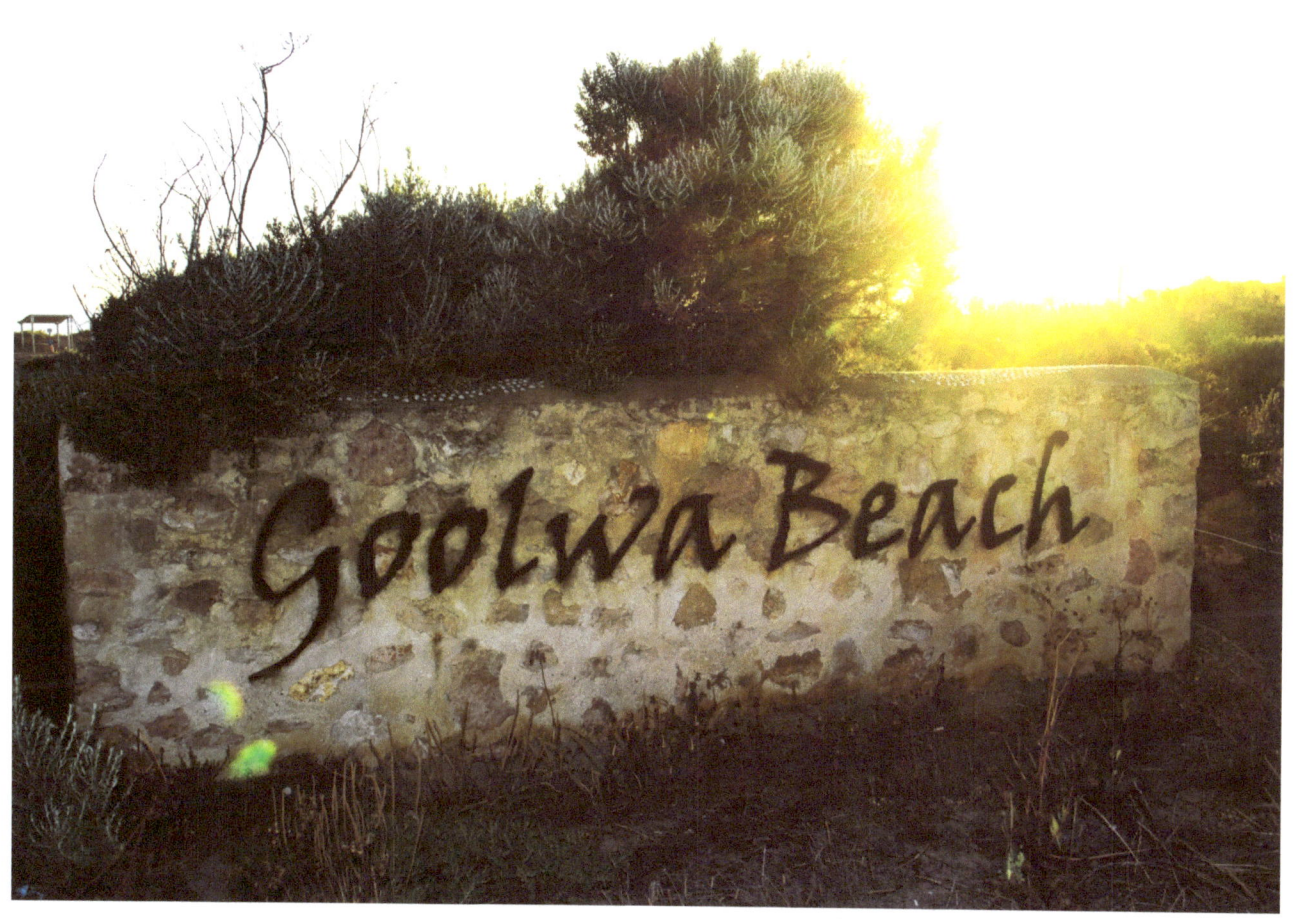

GOOLWA BEACH SIGN

## Goolwa Beach

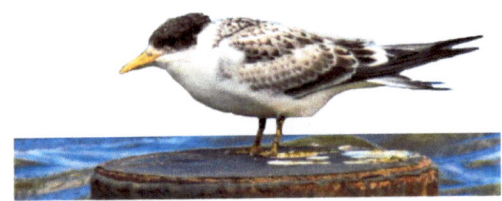

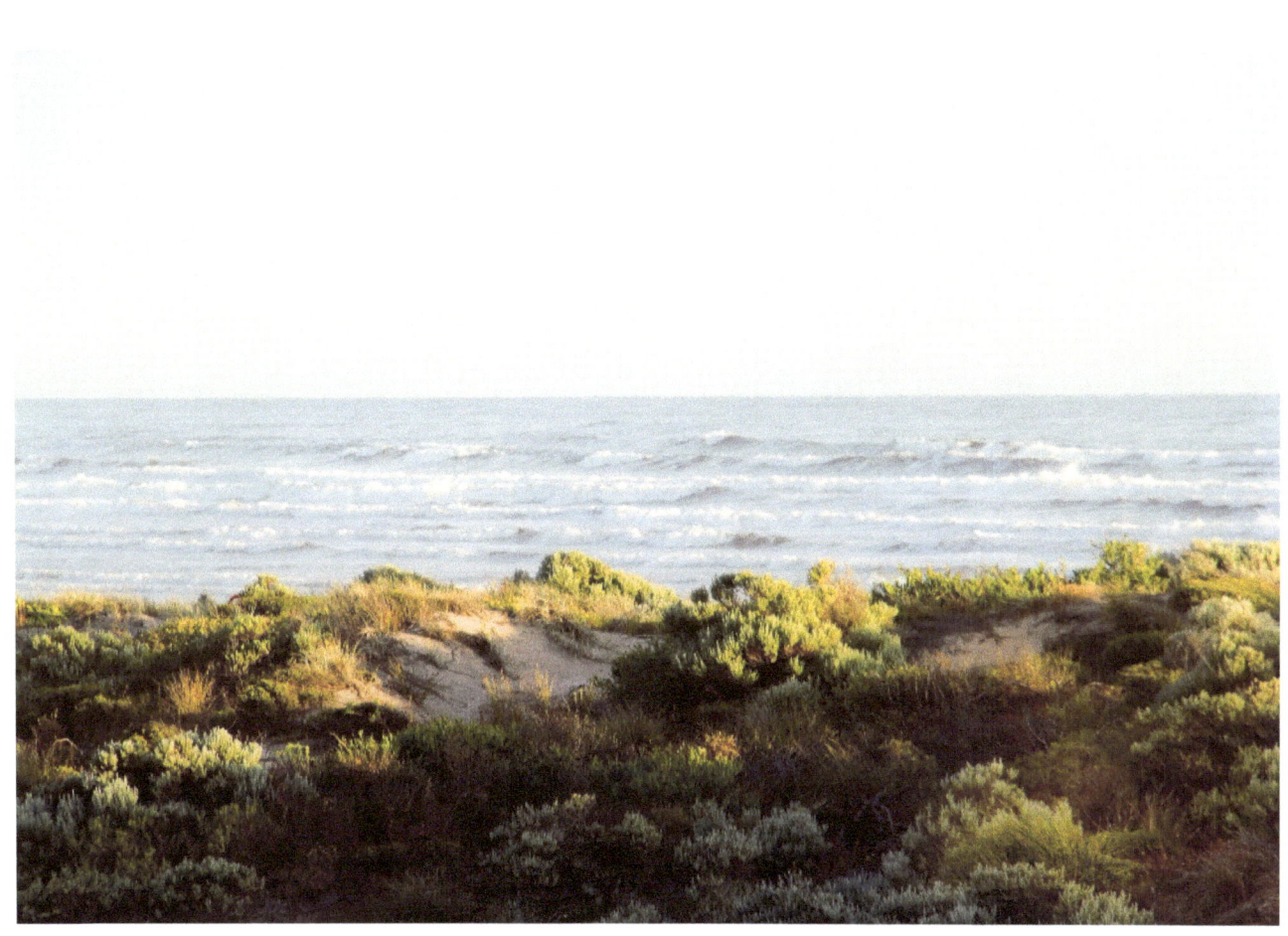

*COORONG NATIONAL PARK SAND DUNE WALK*

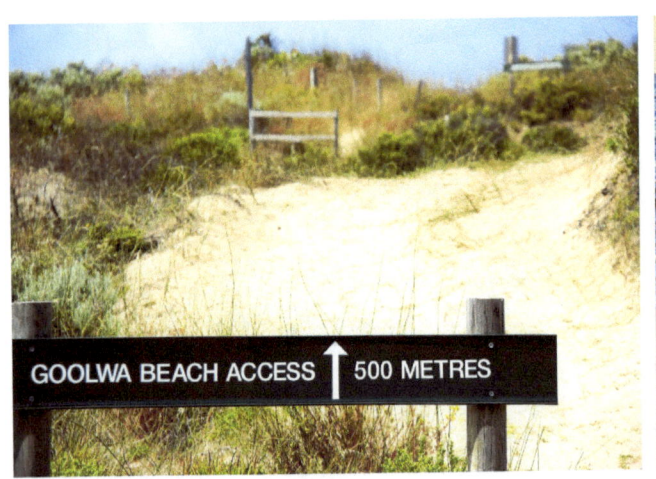 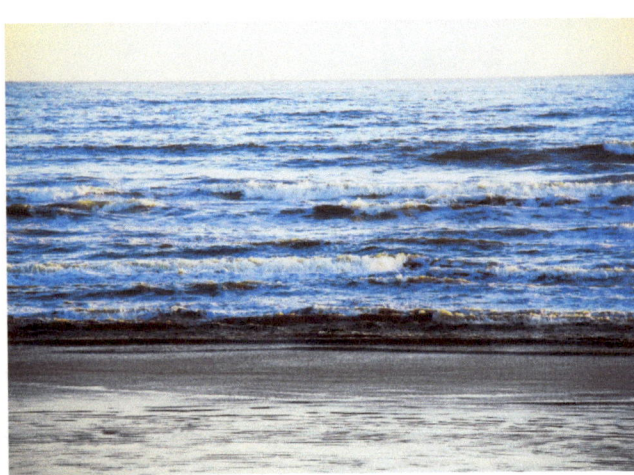

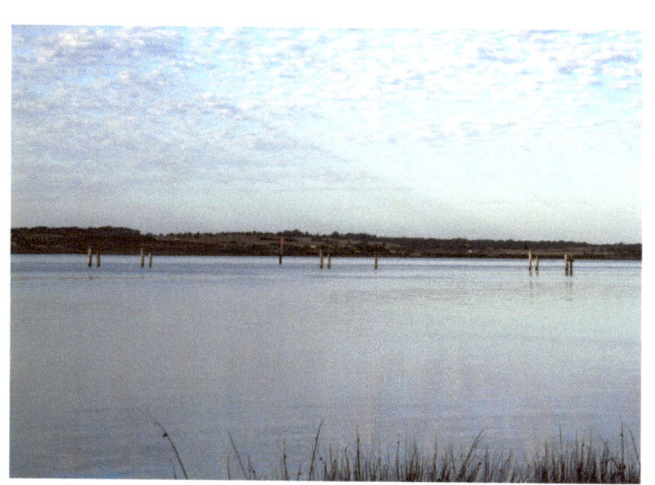 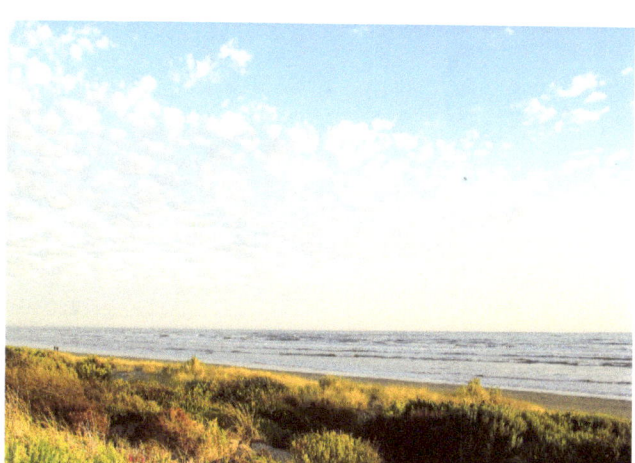

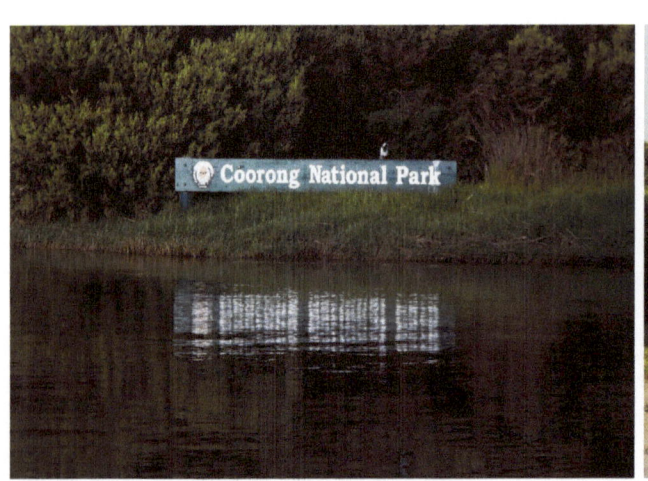
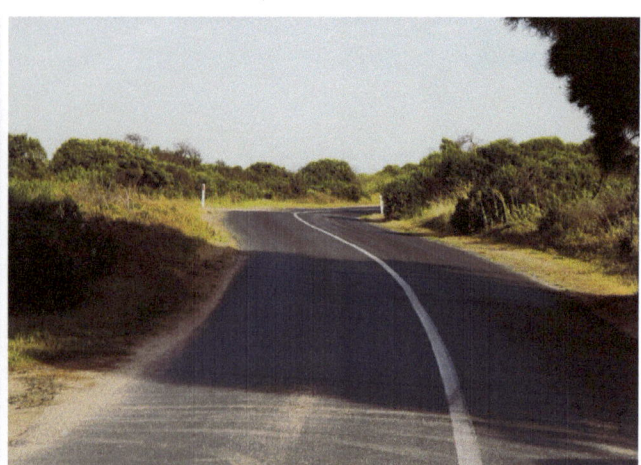

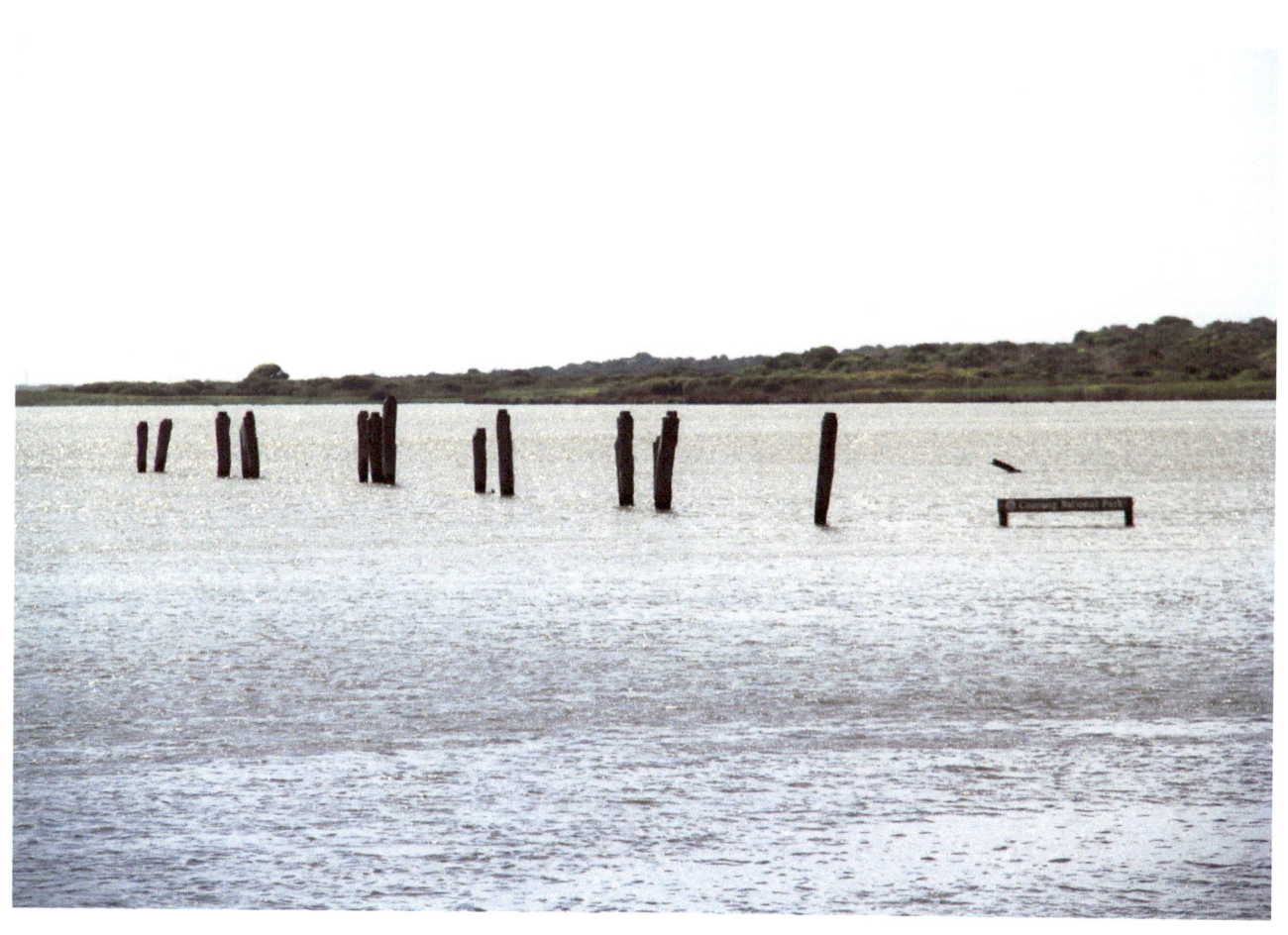

*COORONG NATIONAL PARK SUBMERGED SIGN*

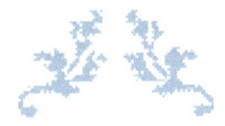

## Coorong National Park

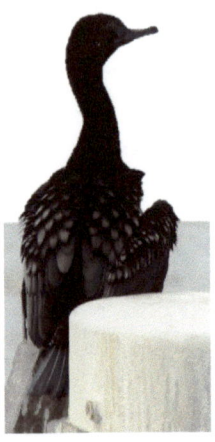

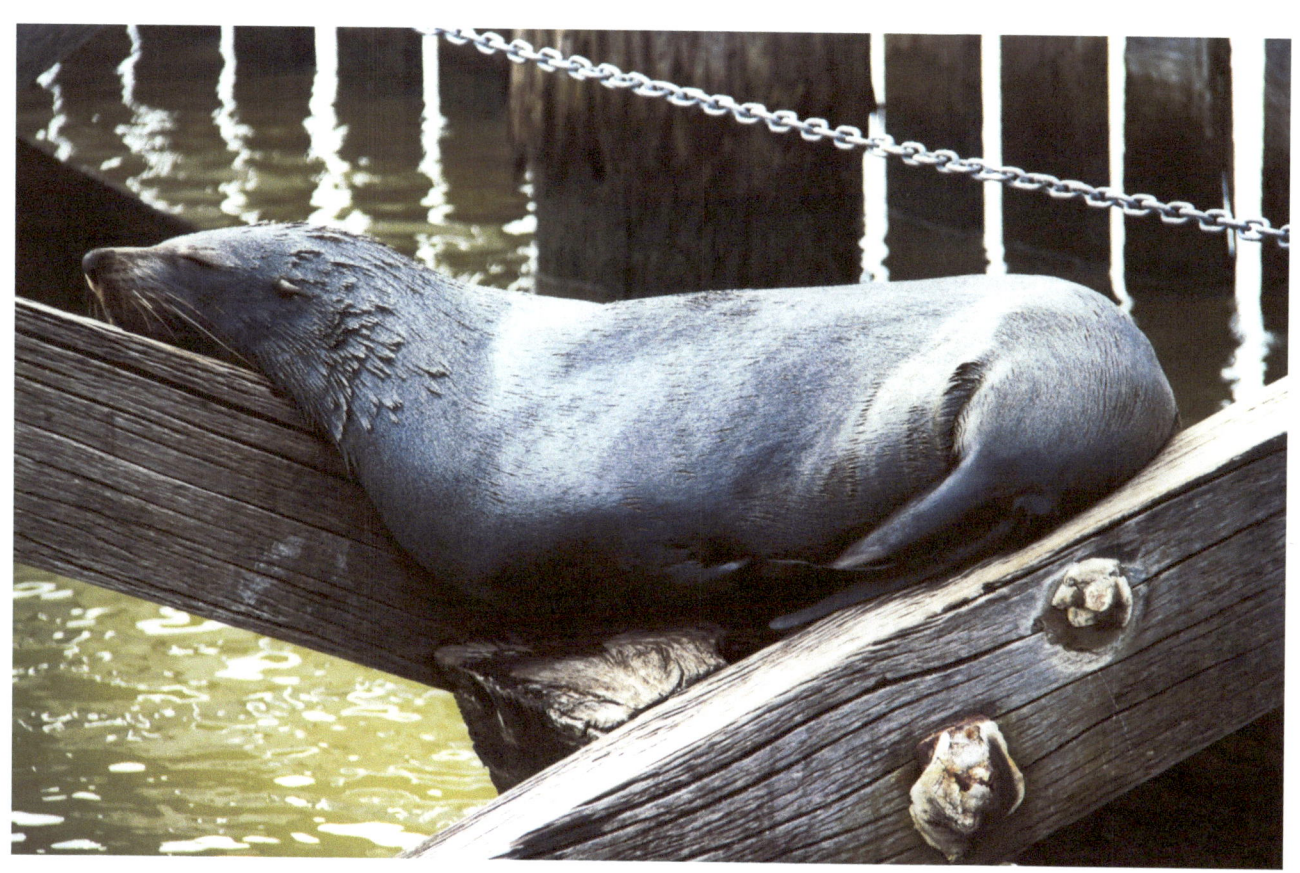

*LOCAL SEAL SLEEPING ON THE LOCK*

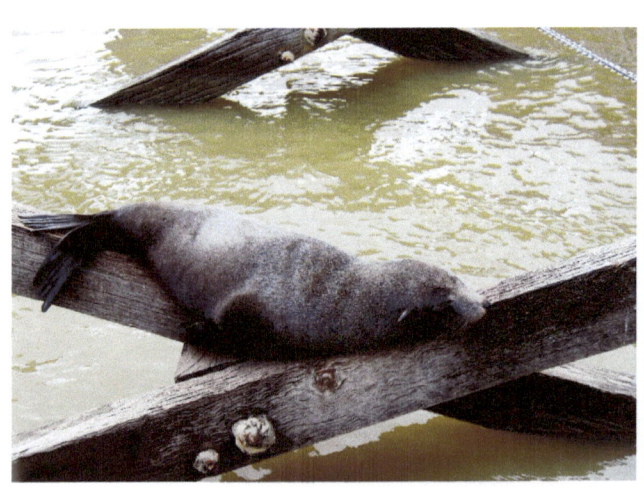 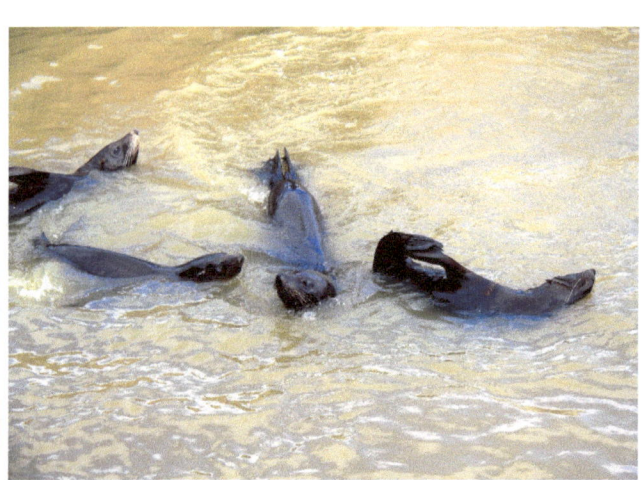

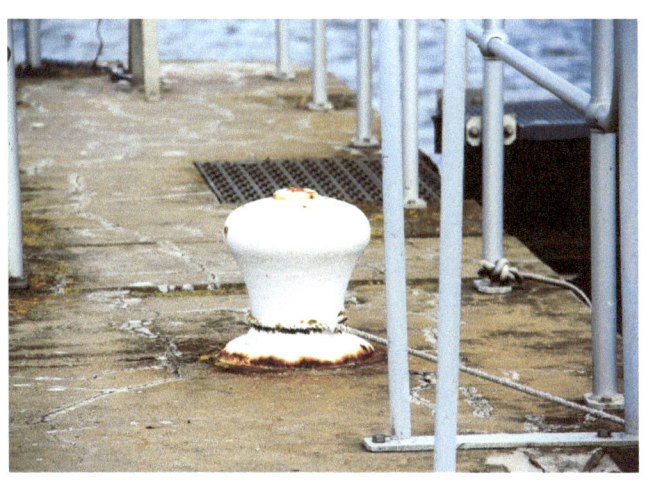 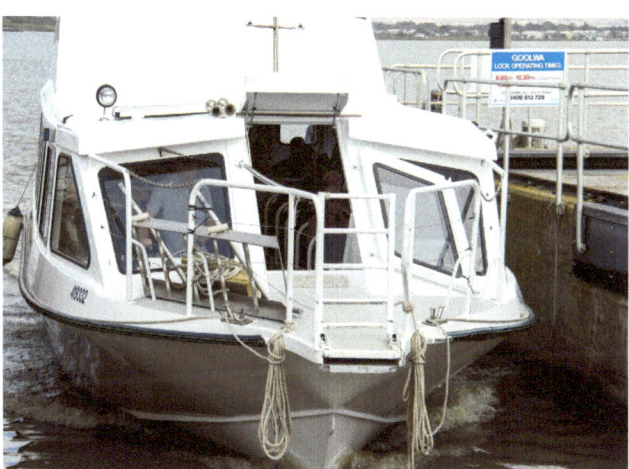

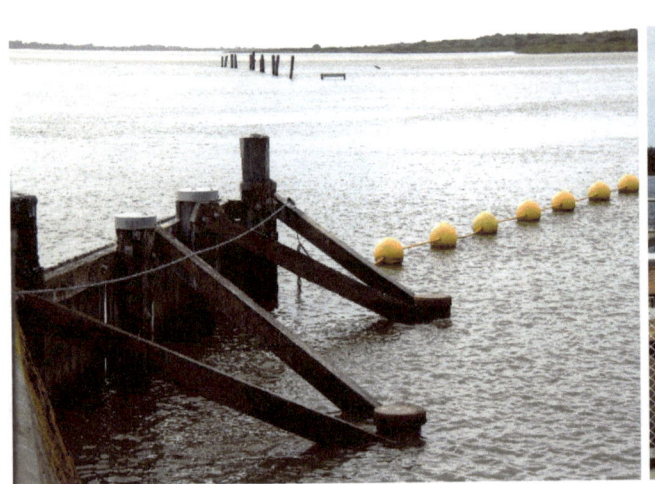 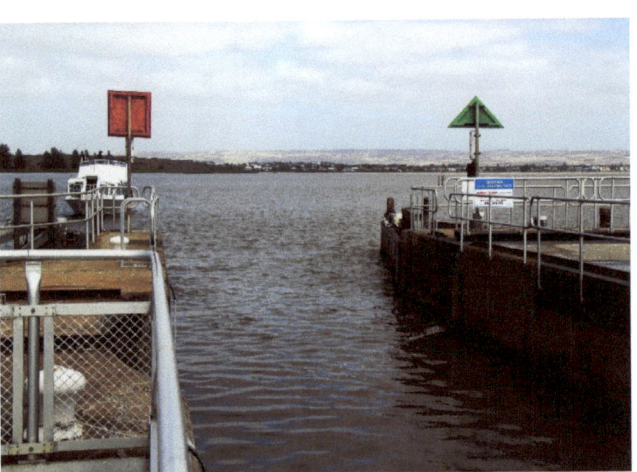

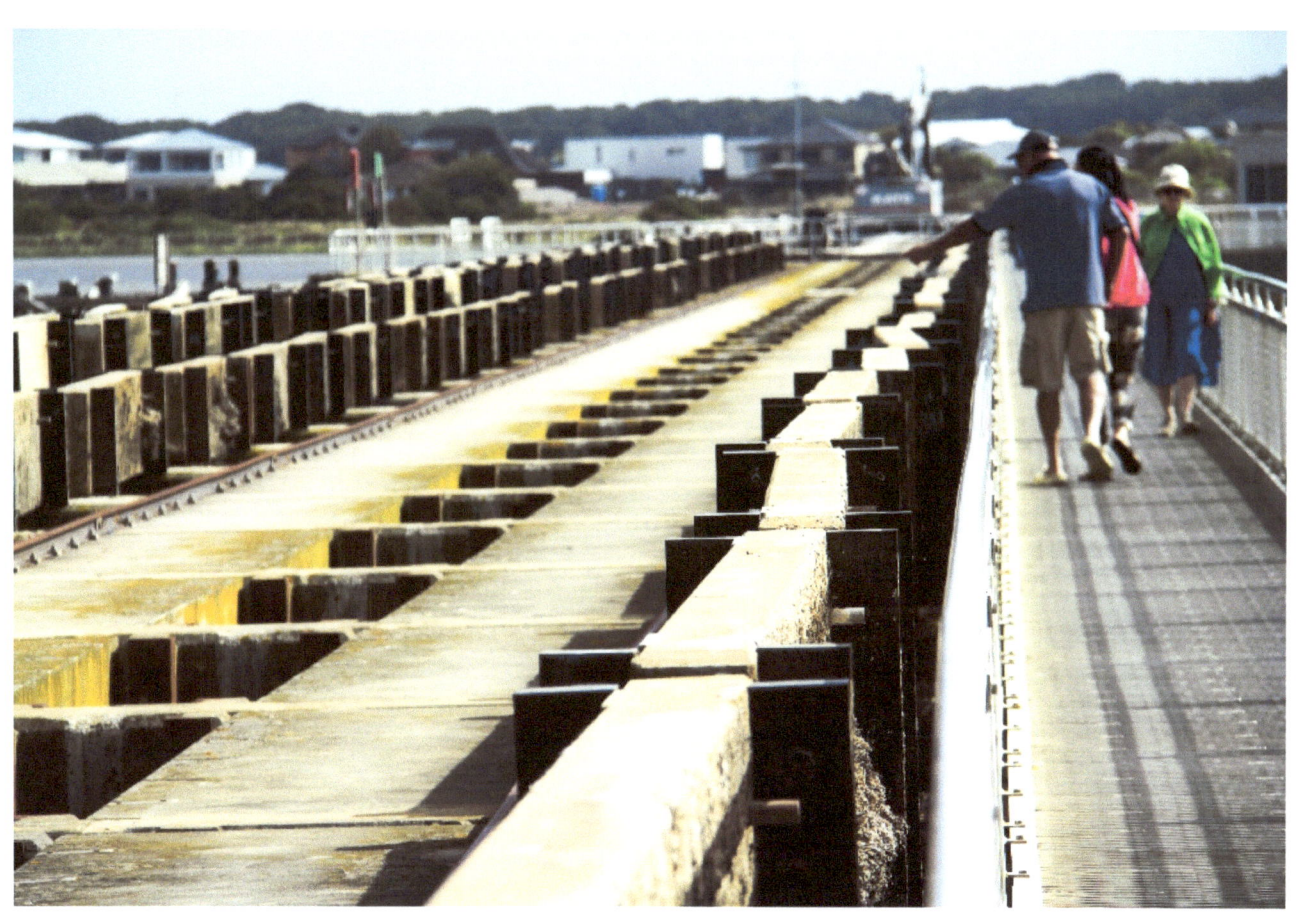

*WALKING ON THE BARRAGE*

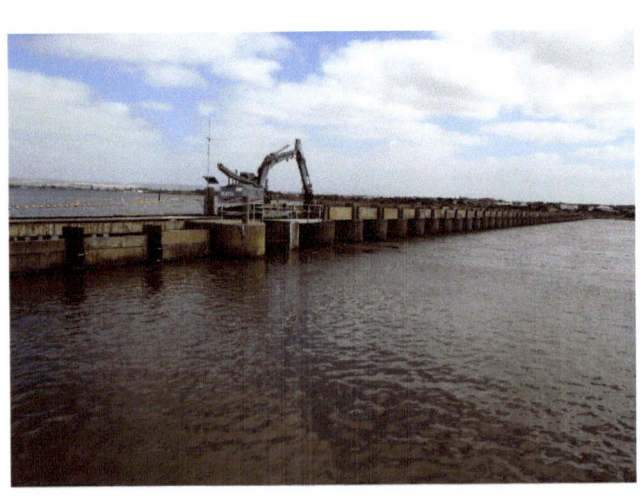
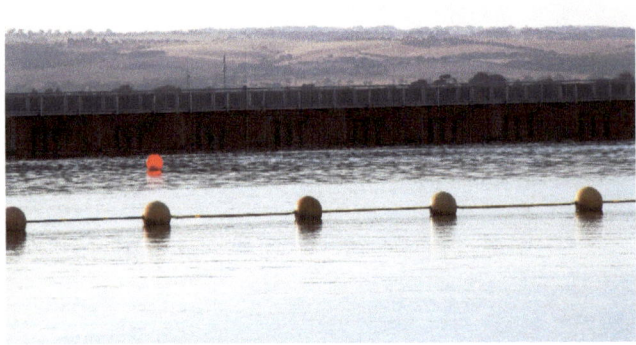

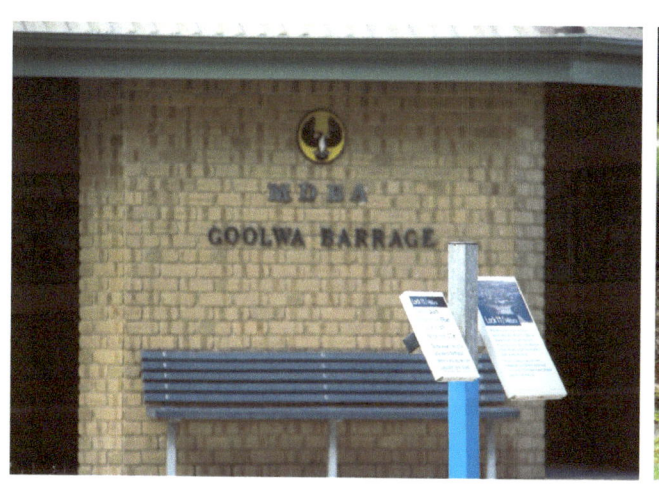 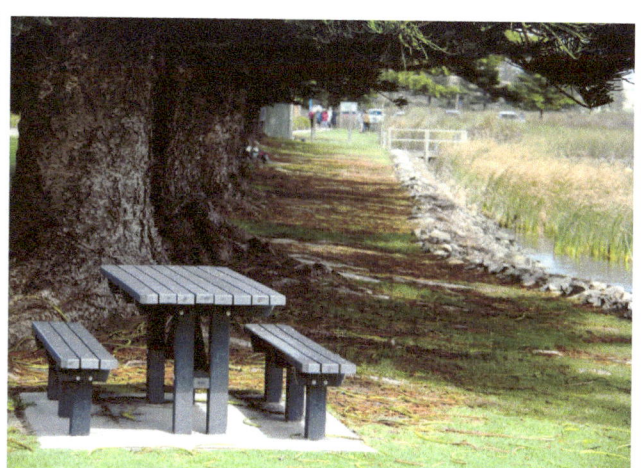

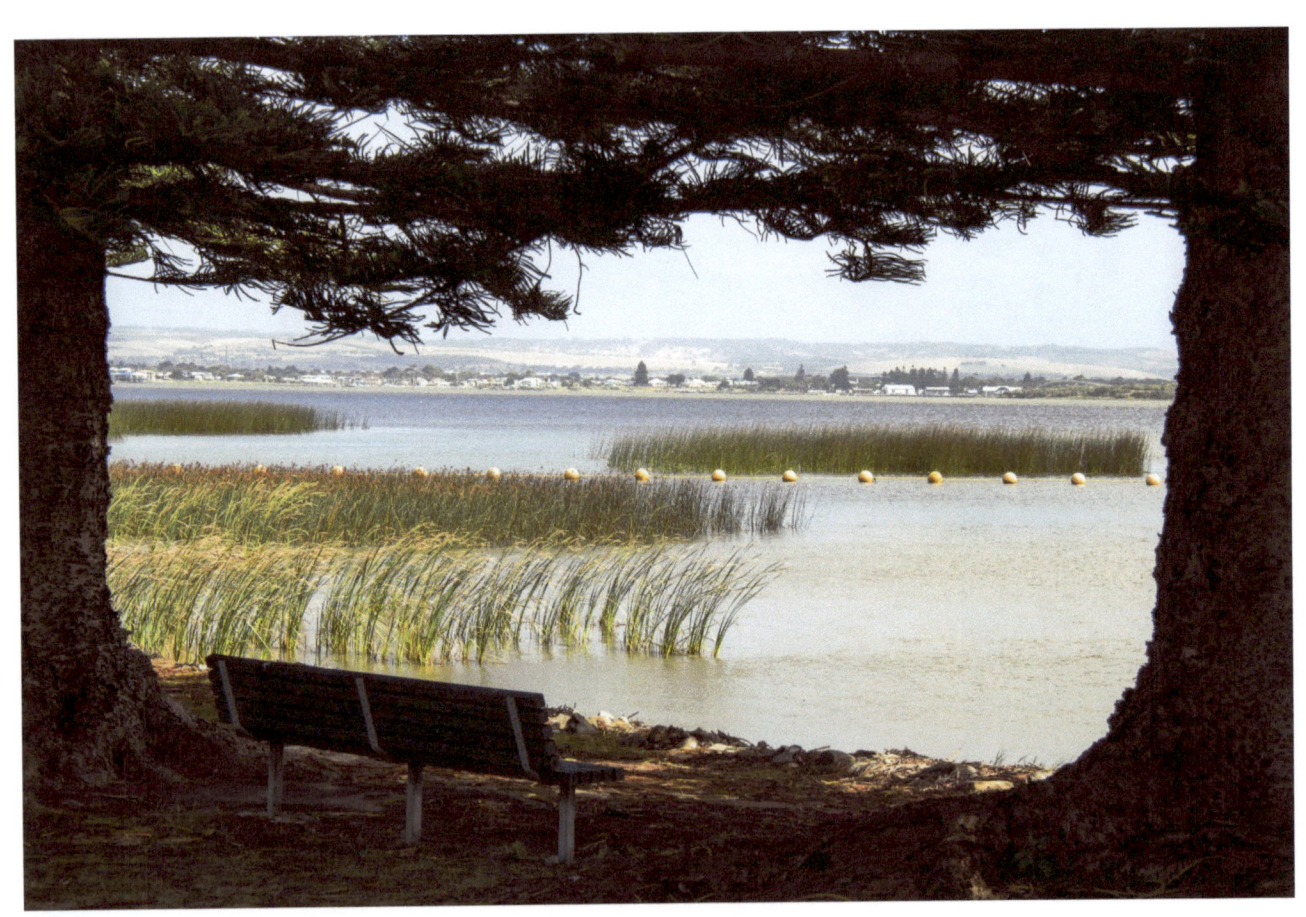

GOOLWA IN THE DISTANCE

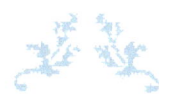

## Goolwa Barrage

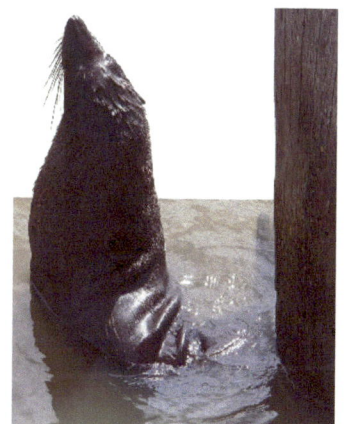

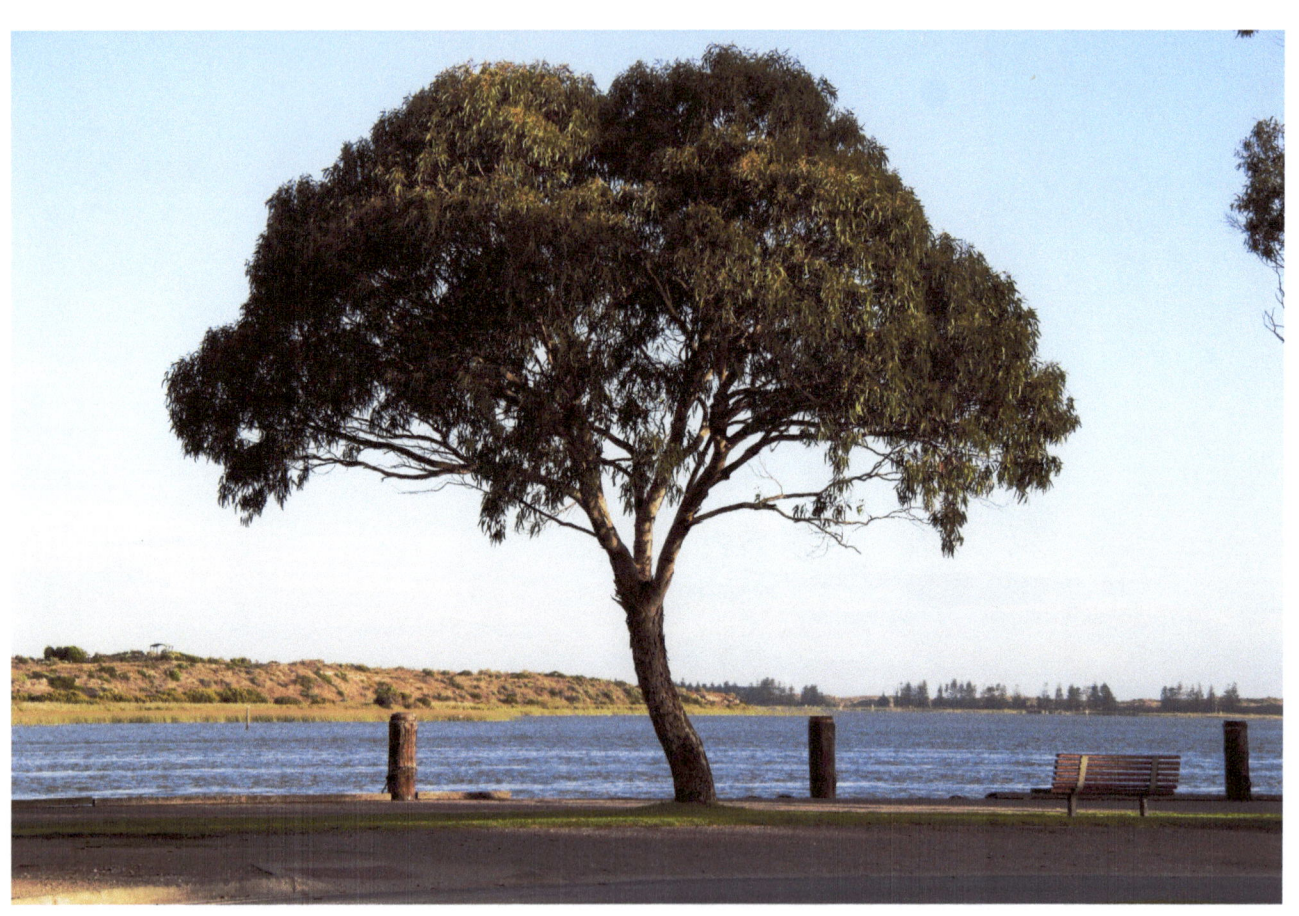

*LOOKING TOWARDS HINDMARSH ISLAND*

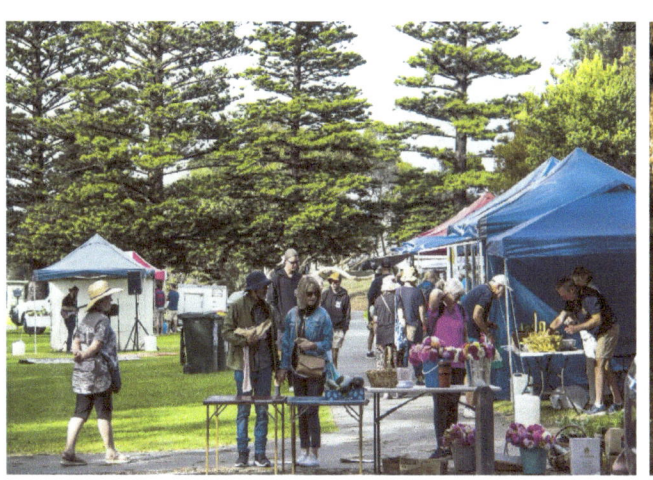 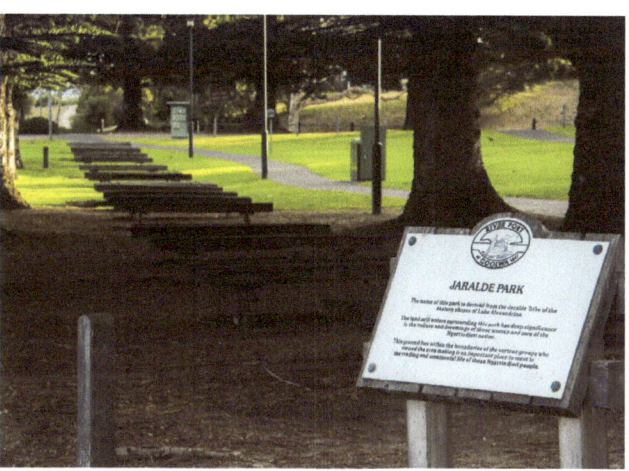

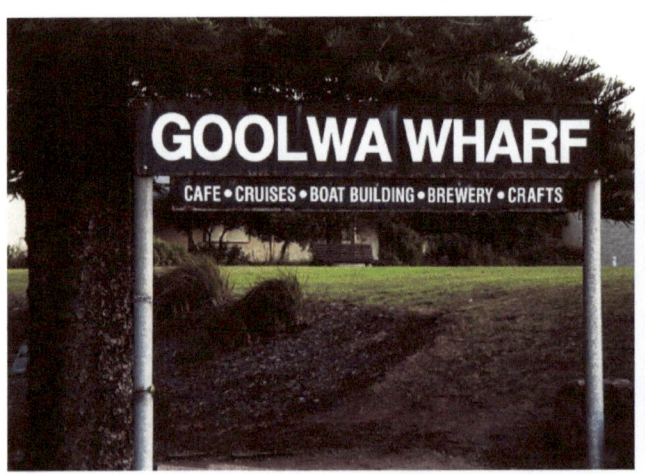 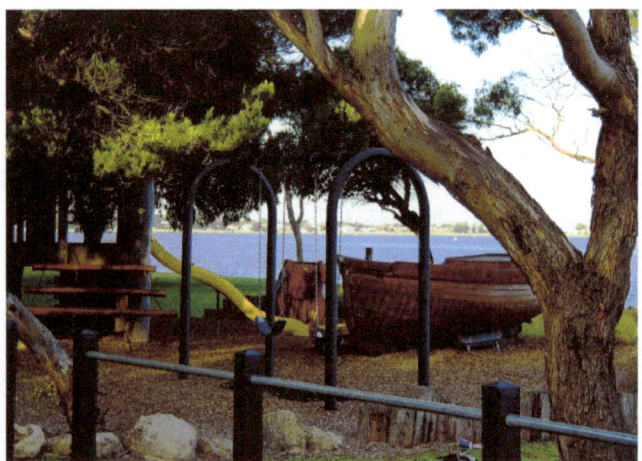

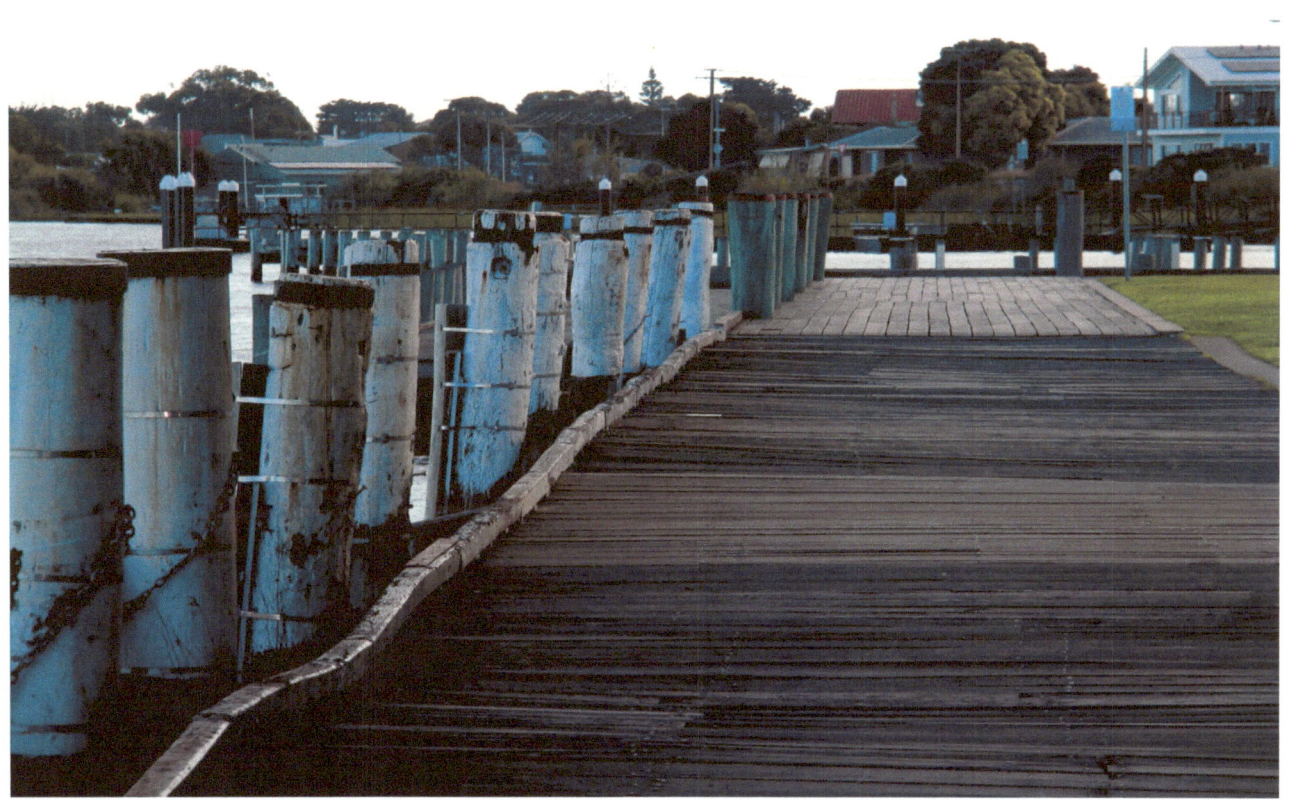

*THE WHARF'S BOAT STOP*

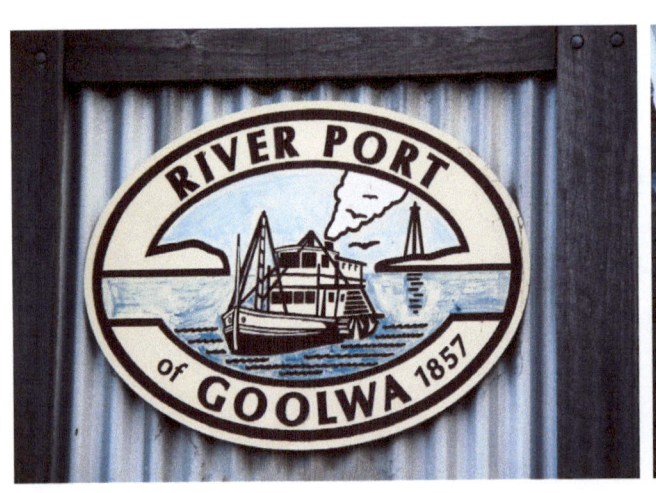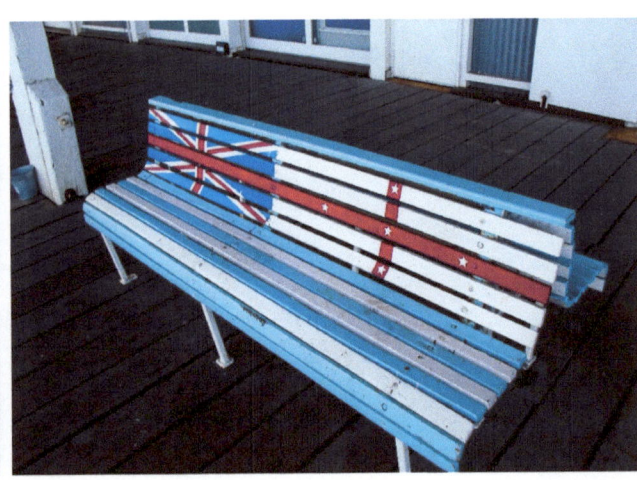

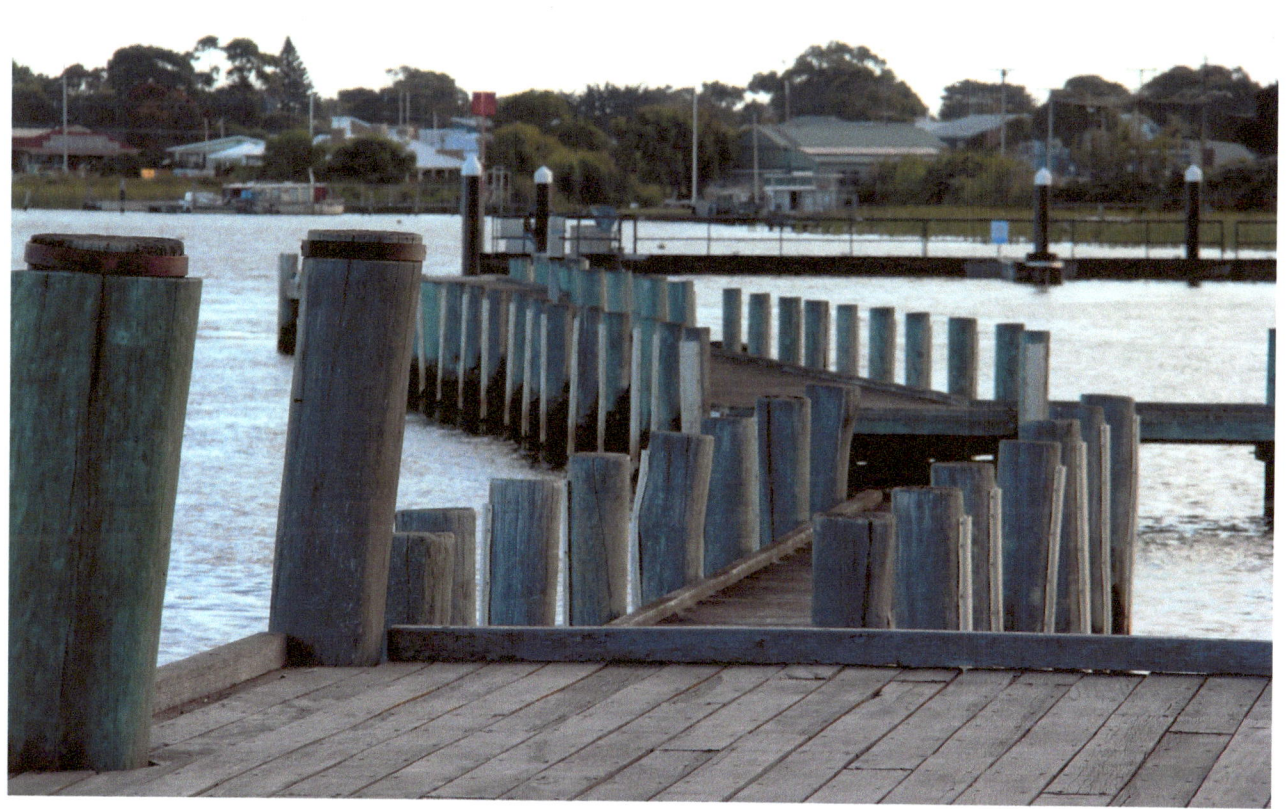

WHARF'S END

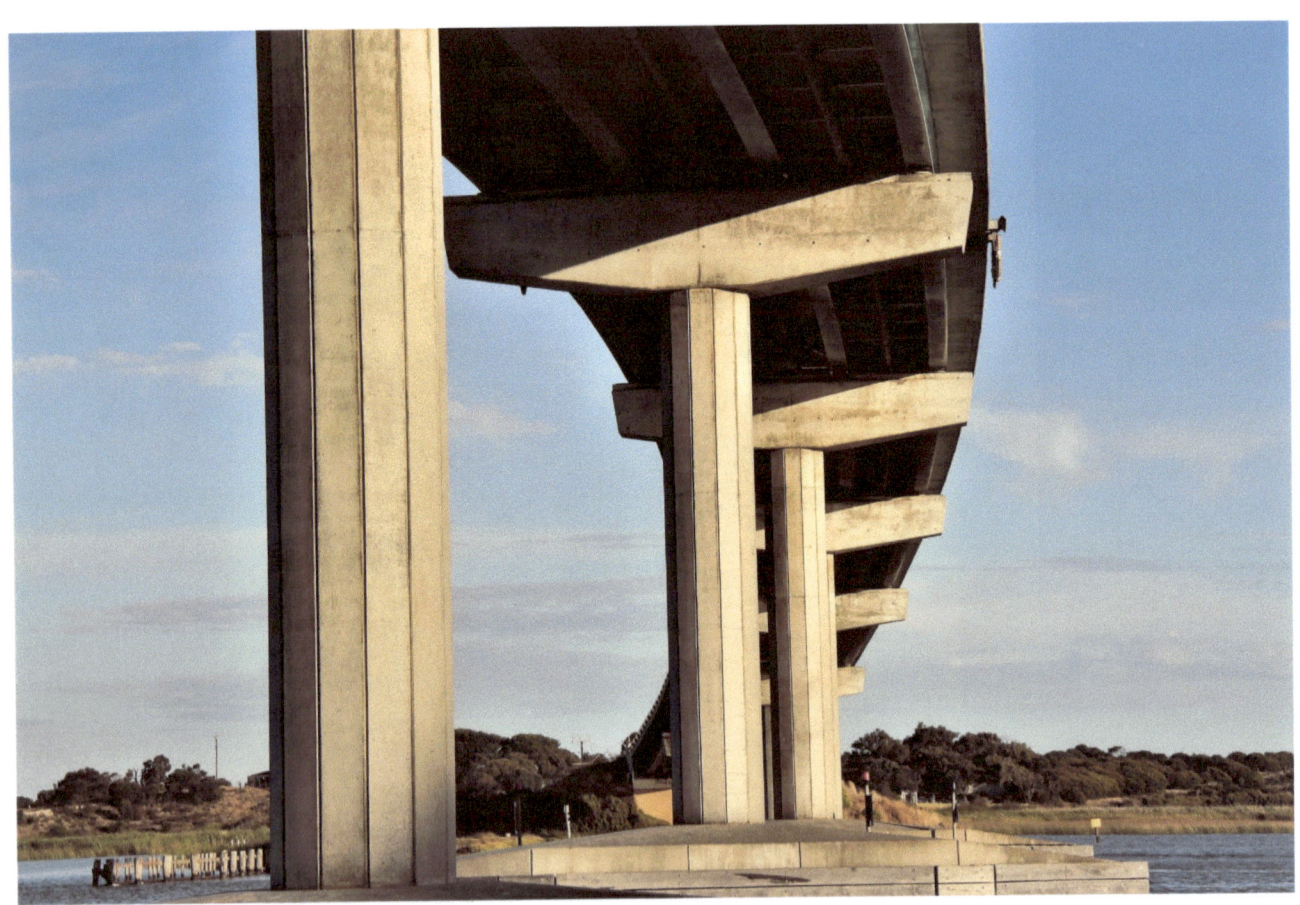

UNDERSIDE OF HINDMARSH ISLAND BRIDGE

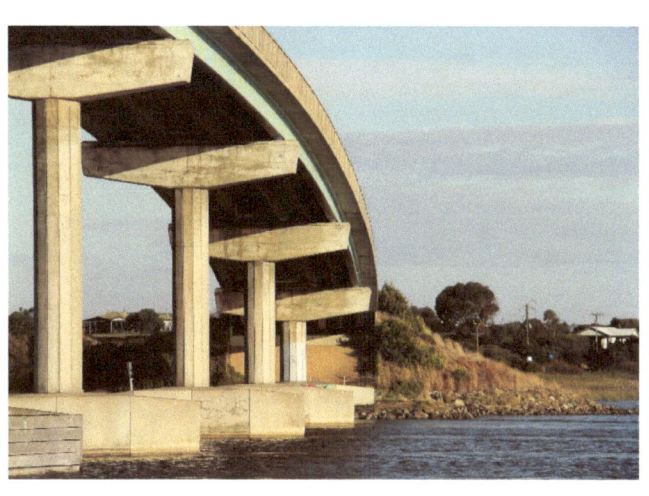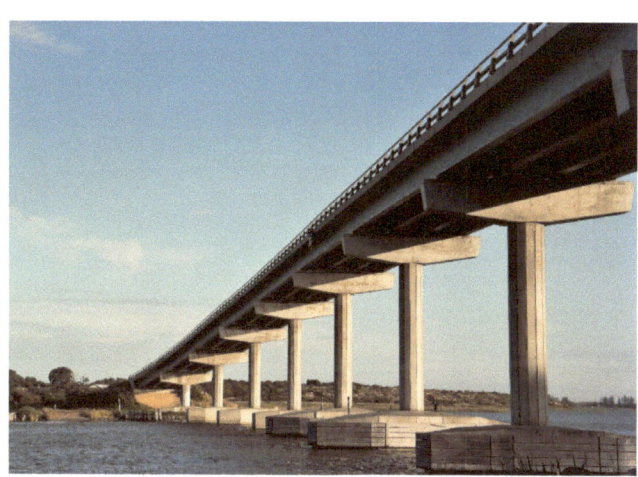

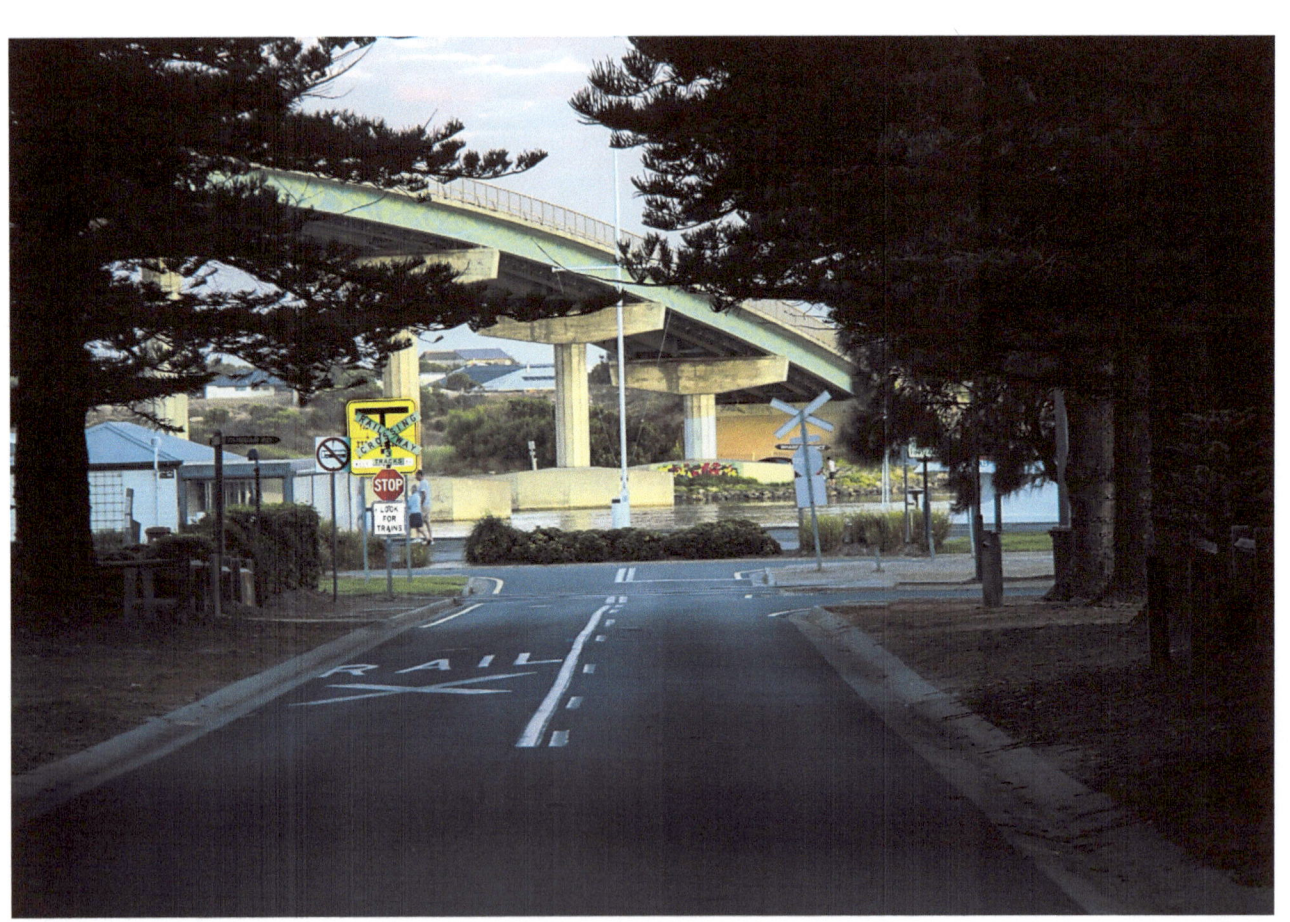

*CUTTING ROAD ENTRANCE*

# Goolwa Wharf

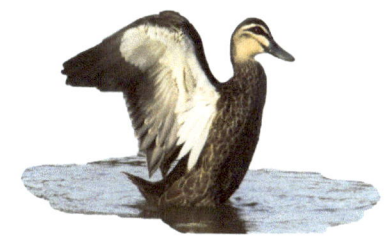

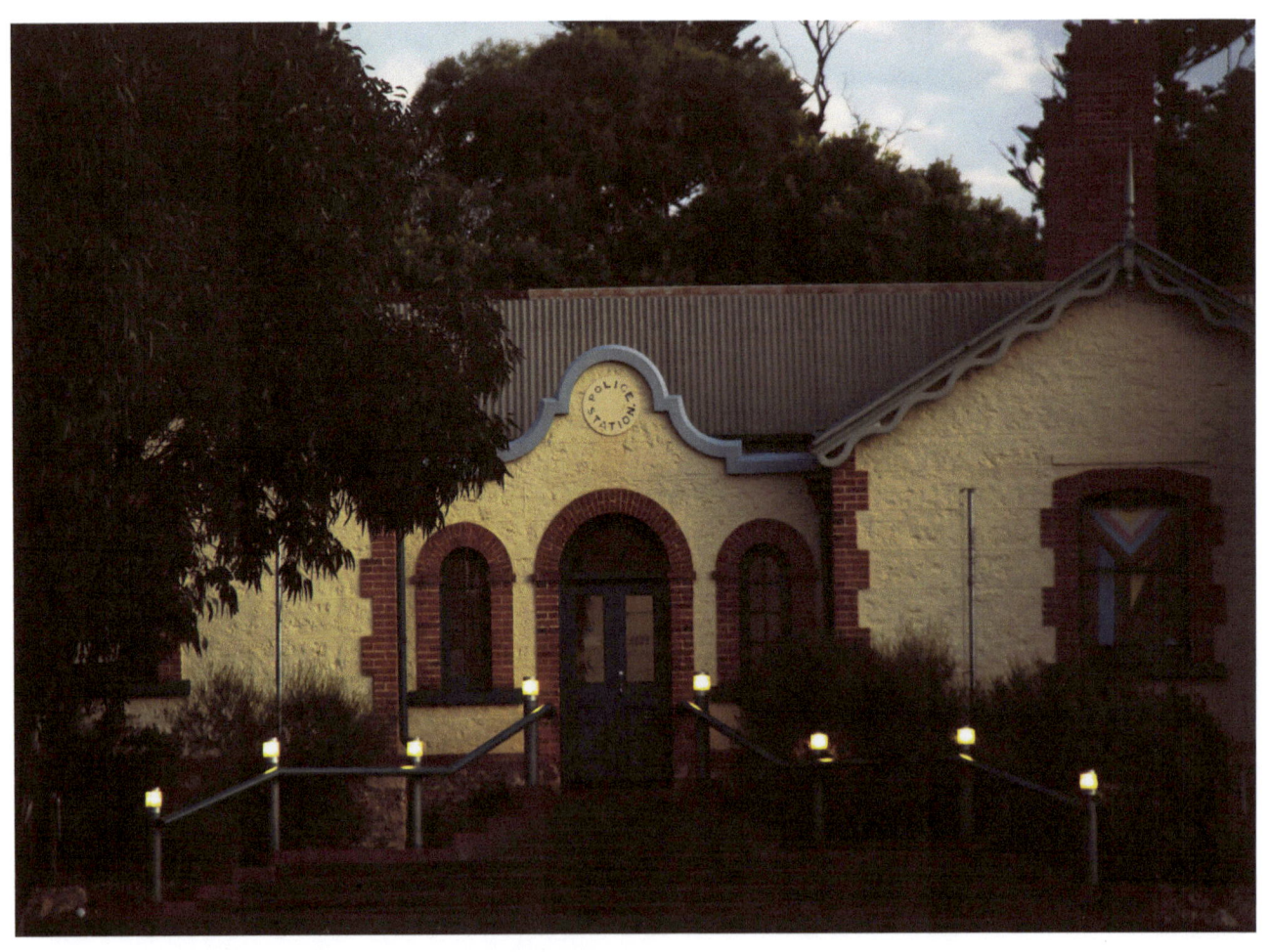

*SOUTH COAST REGIONAL ARTS CENTRE, GOOLWA TERRACE*

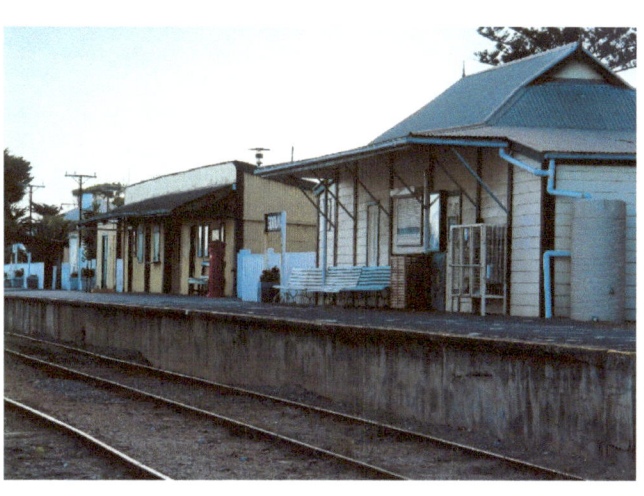 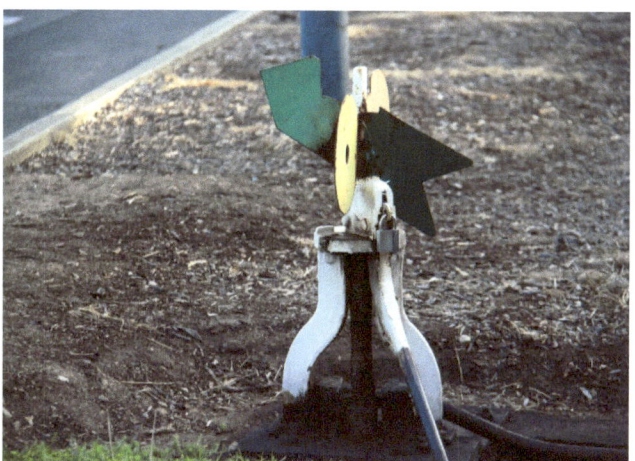

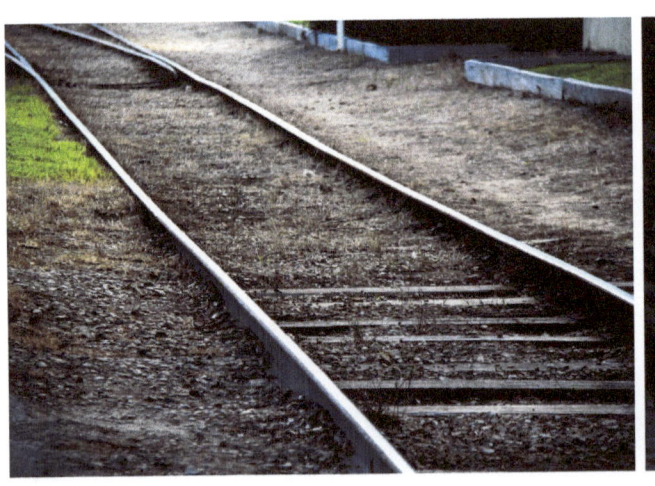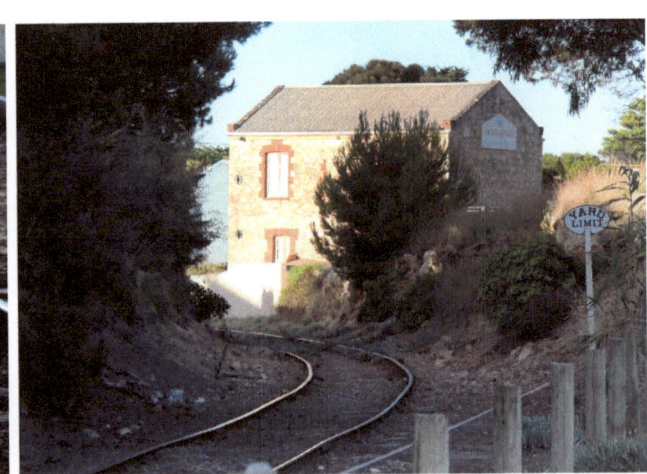

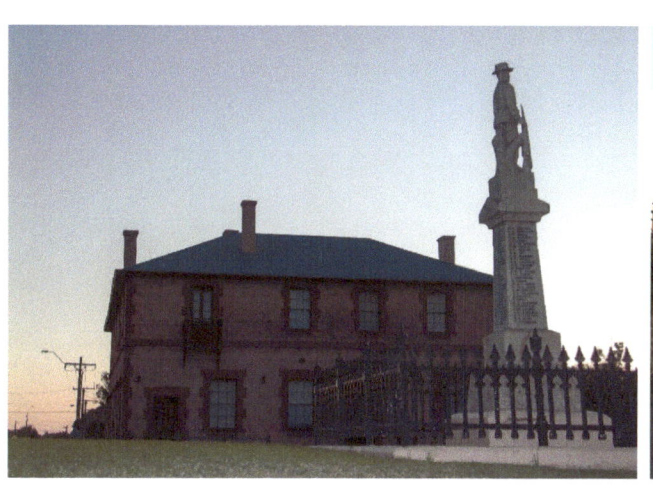
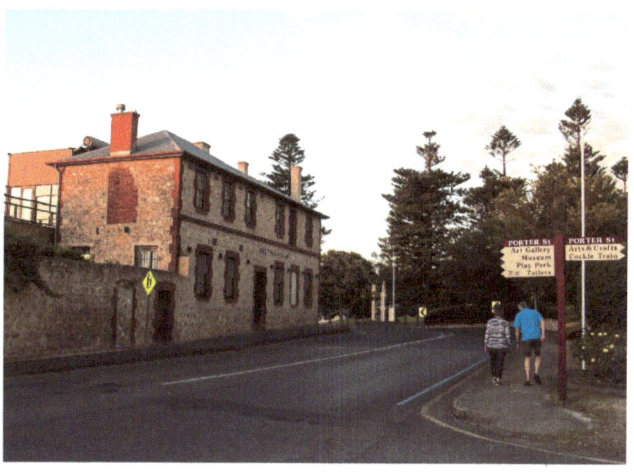

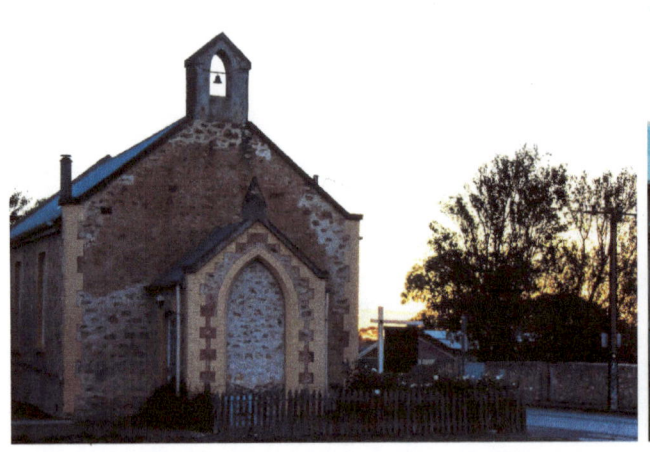
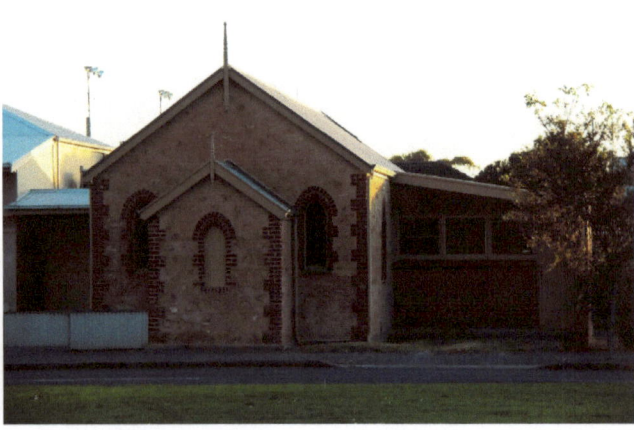

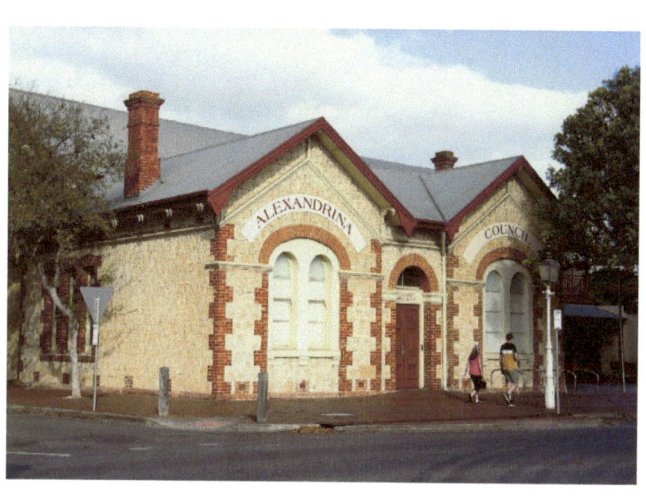 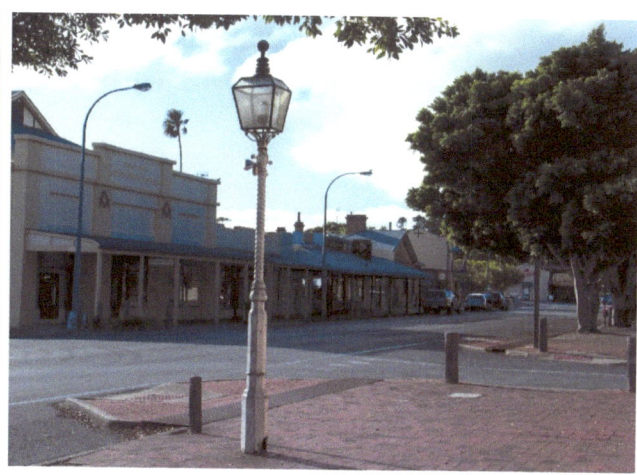

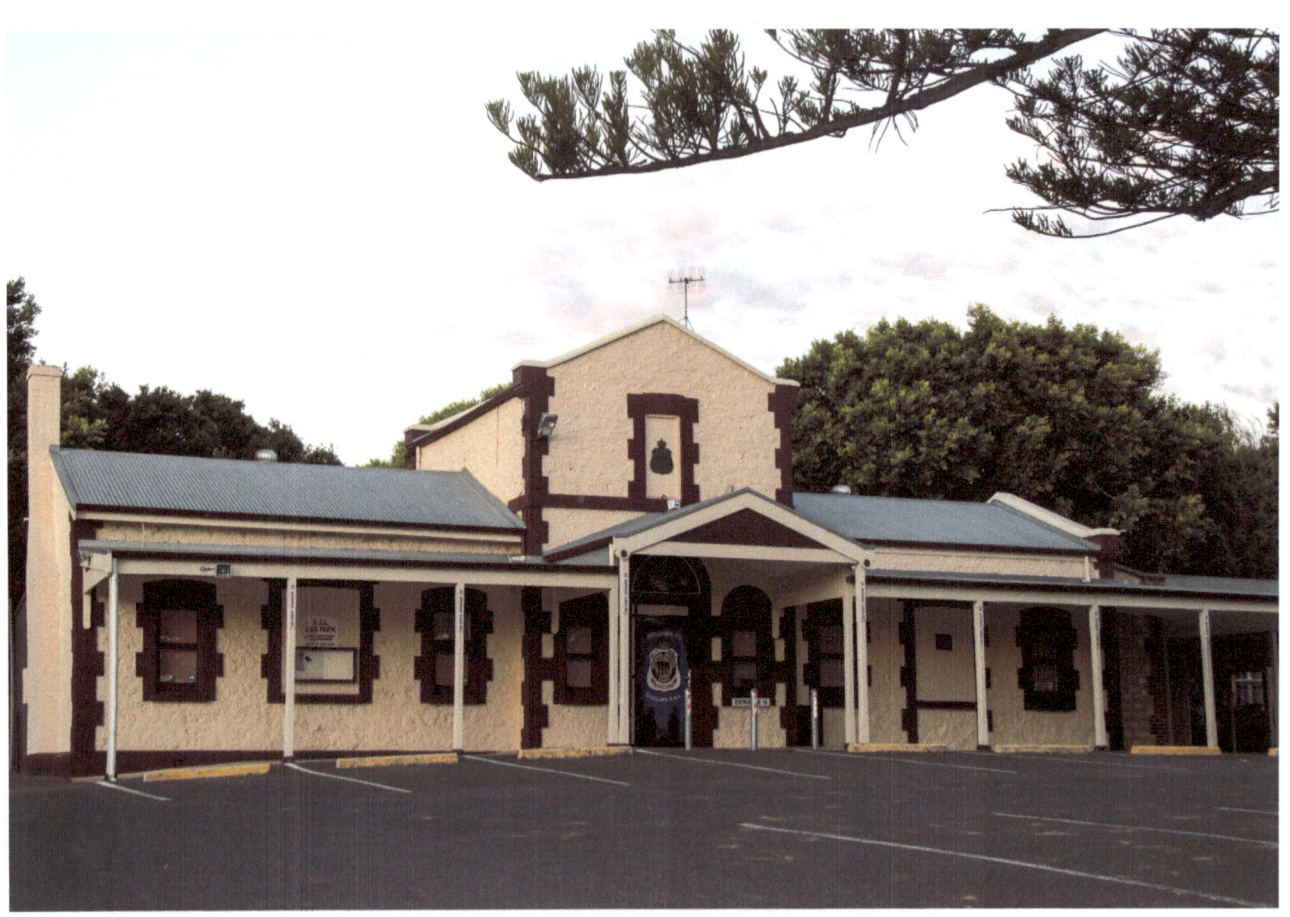

*RSL, CUTTING ROAD*

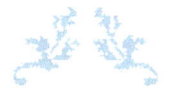

## On The Heritage Track

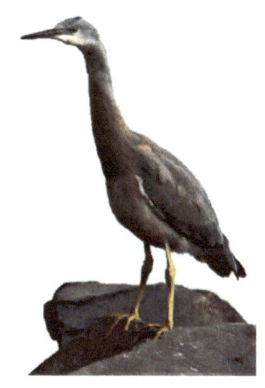

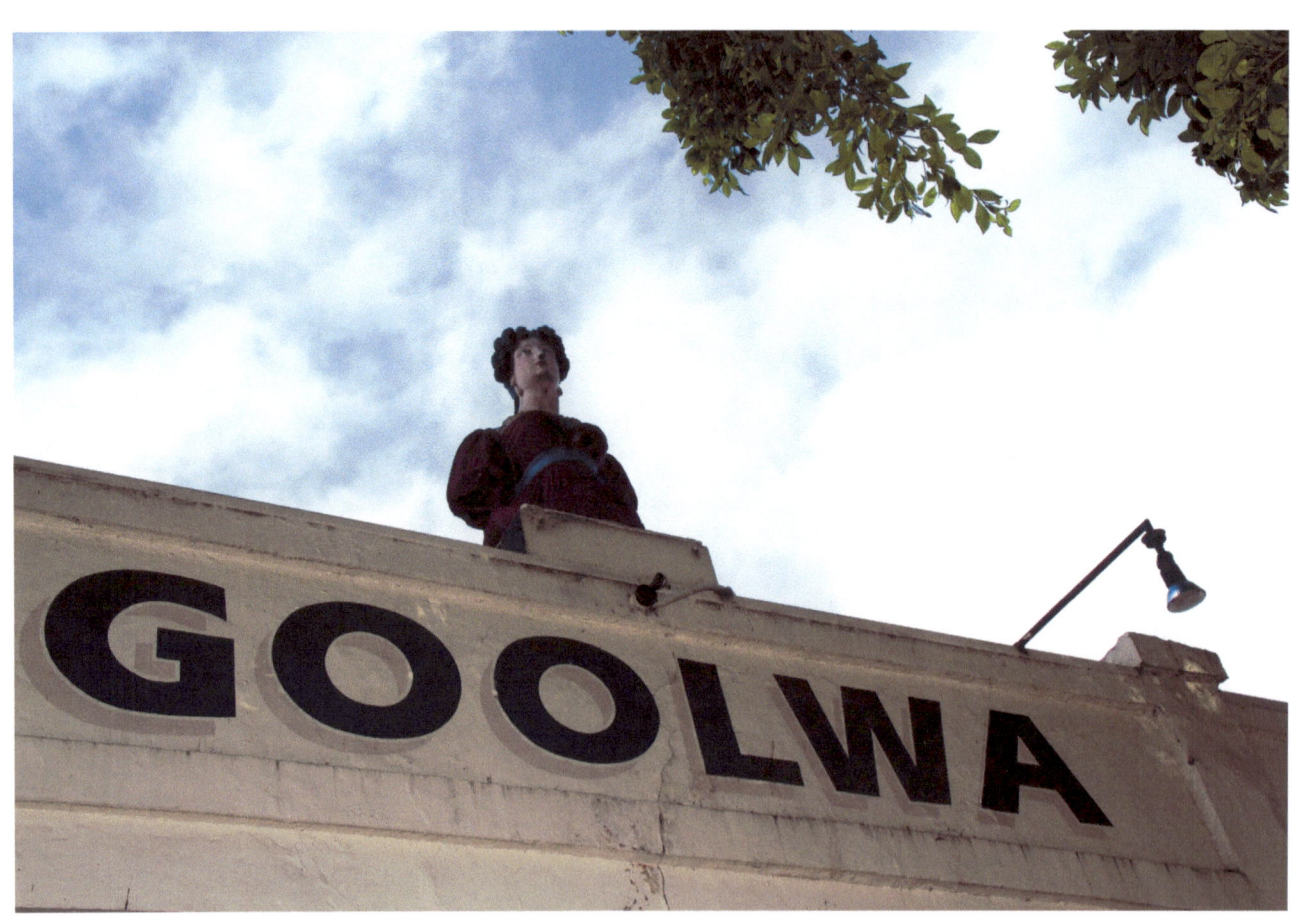

GOOLWA HOTEL, CADELL STREET

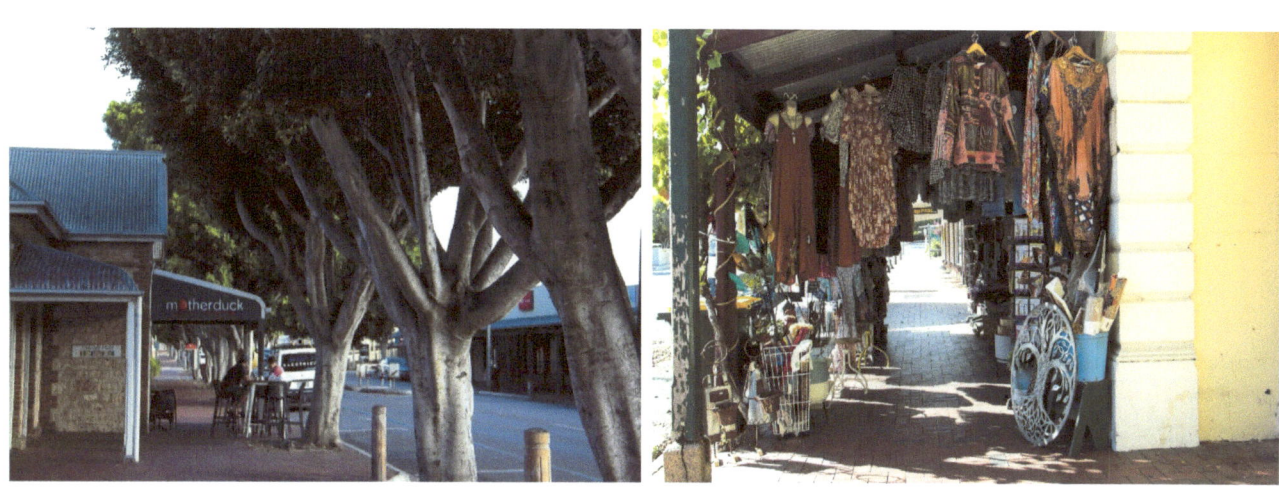

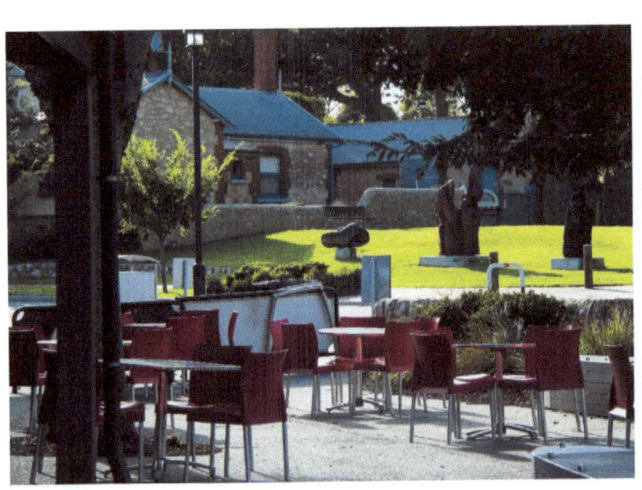
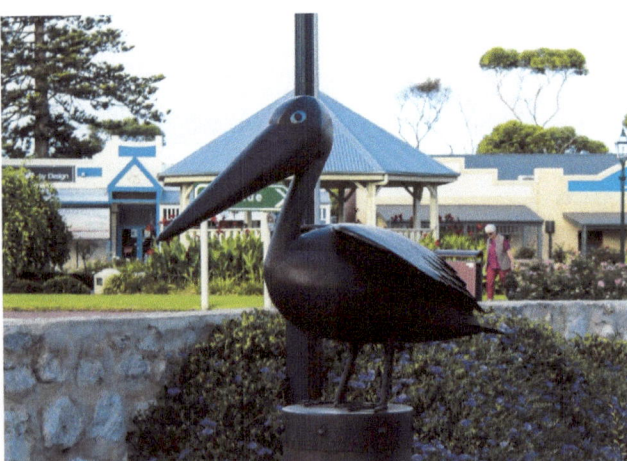

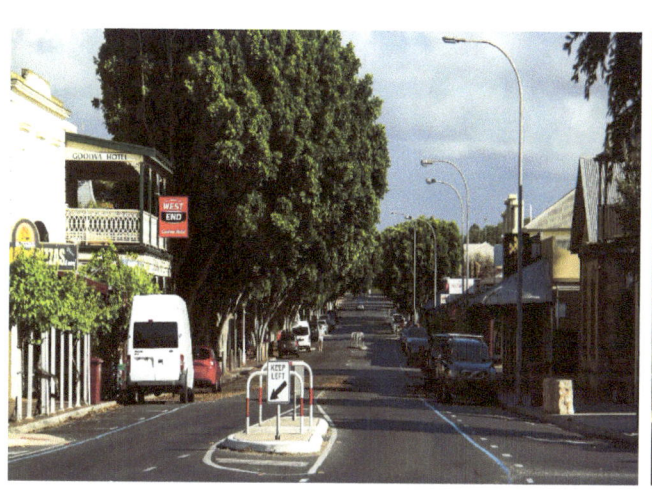 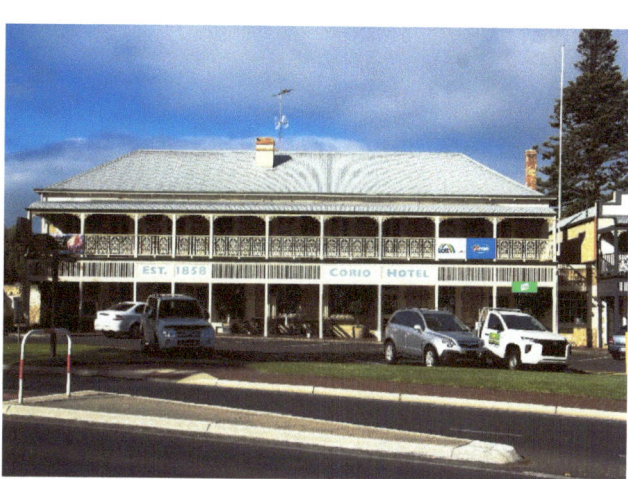

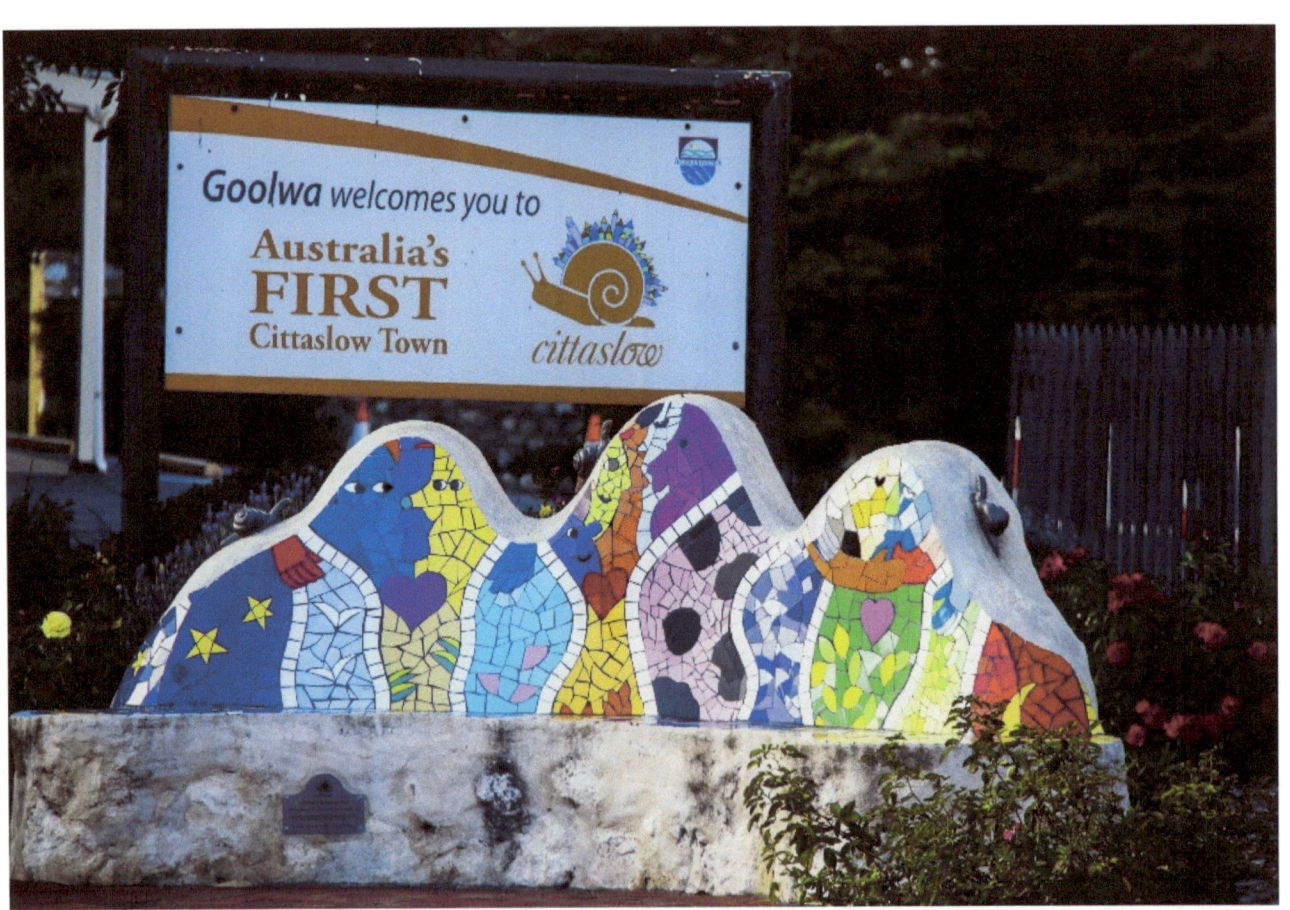

GOOLWA TERRACE

## Goolwa Main Street

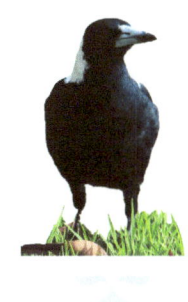

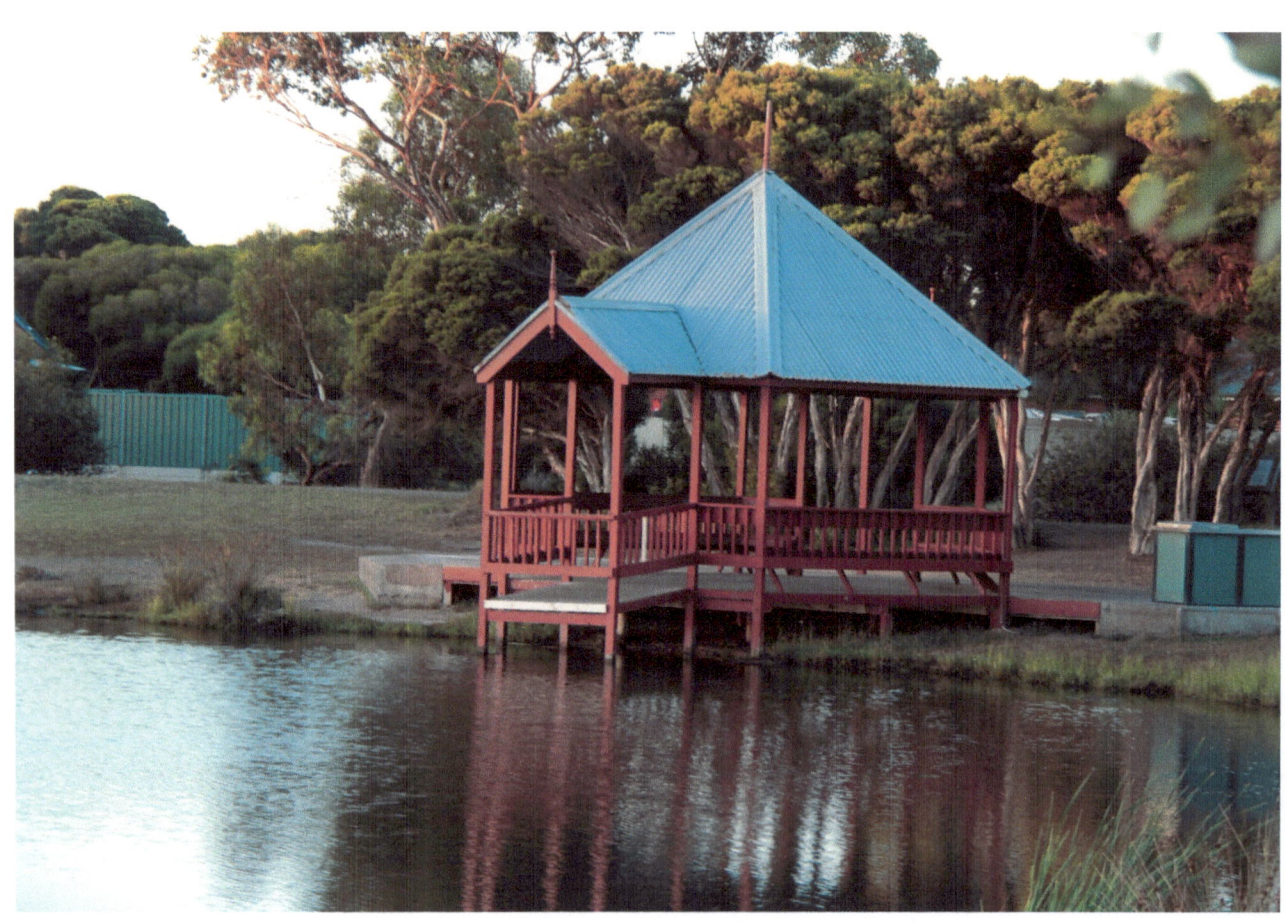

*MURRAY SMITH PARK, DAWSON STREET*

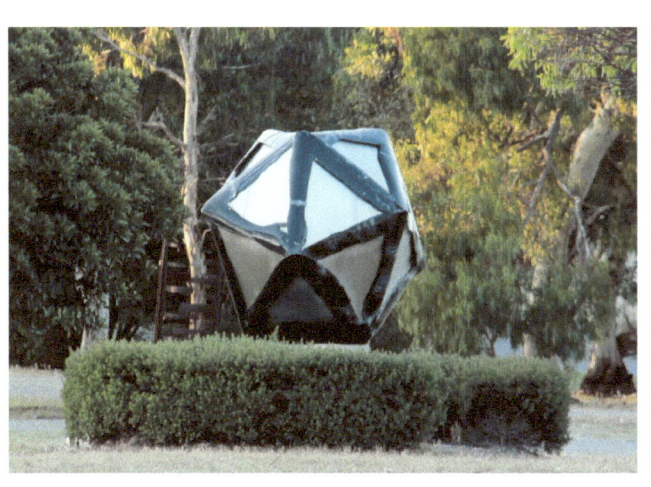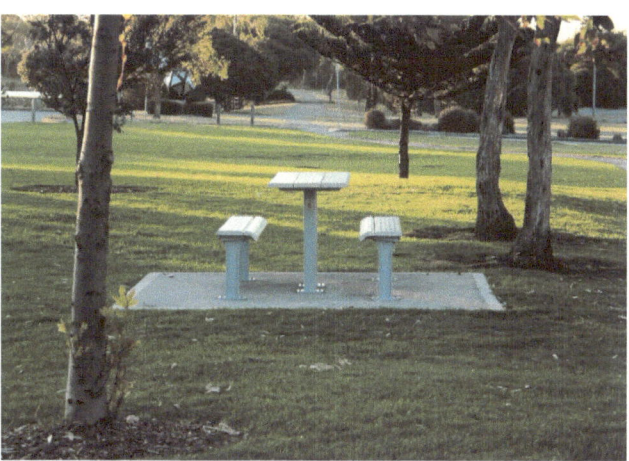

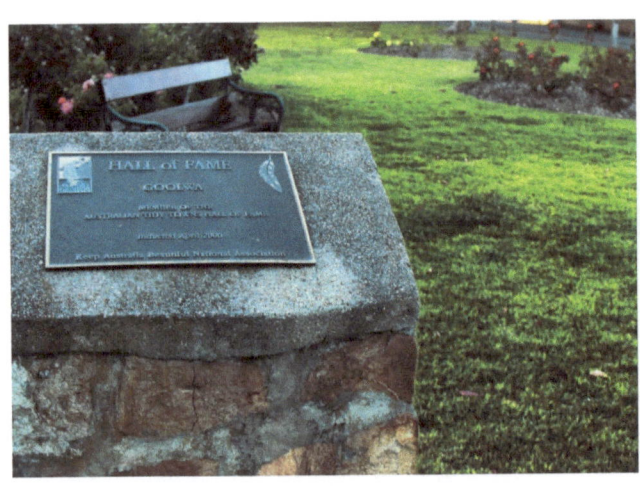
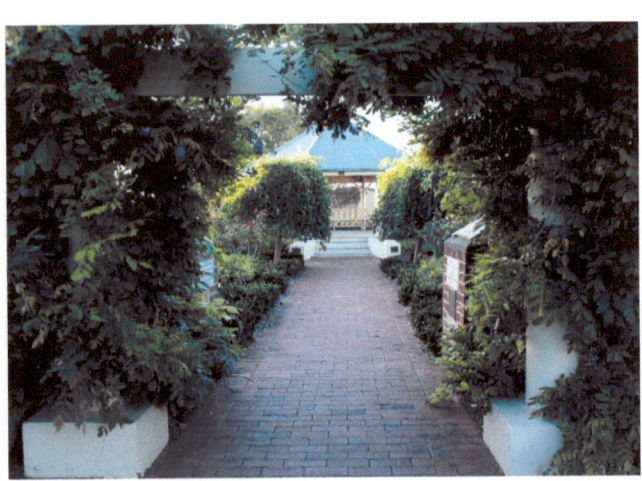

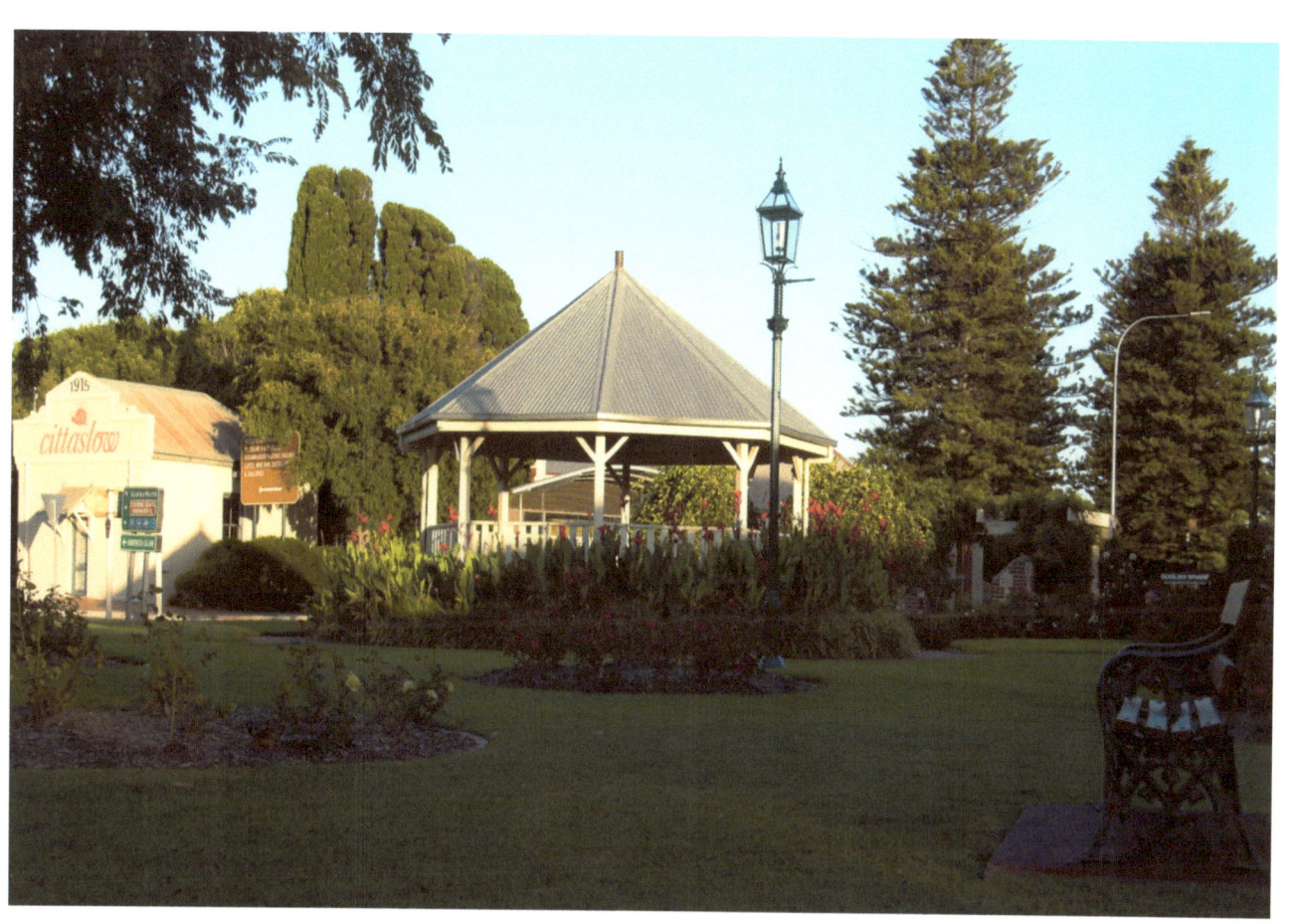

*ARTHUR NEIGHBOUR RESERVE, CADELL STREET*

## Goolwa Town Parks

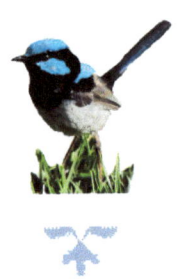

Digital Media has been a passion of mine for as long as I can remember. As a photographer, I am constantly searching for new and inspiring places to capture through my lens. And when it comes to beautiful and unique locations, Goolwa holds a special place in my heart.

I was first drawn to Goolwa's stunning natural beauty - from the serene waters of the Murray River to the sandy coastline and beautiful beaches. But as I began to explore the town and its surrounds, I discovered so much more. The rich history, the vibrant local community, the quaint cafes and boutique shops - all these elements came together to create a truly special place.

Through my photographs, I aim to capture the essence of Goolwa - to share its beauty, its character, and its spirit with the world. Each image is carefully crafted to showcase the unique features that make this town so special, from the stunning scenery to the historic houses around the main street.

Ultimately, I chose to photograph places in Goolwa because I believe that this town deserves to be celebrated and shared with the world. It is a place of beauty, history, and community, and I feel privileged to be able to capture its charm through my lens. I hope that this book will inspire others to explore Goolwa for themselves, and to discover the magic that I have found in this special corner of South Australia.


L. Sanders

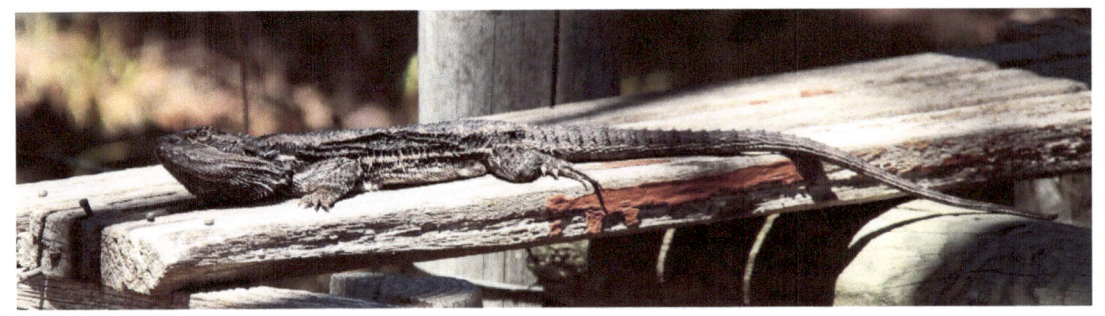

# Hot Spot Photos
# 2023

*By L. Sanders*

## DEDICATION

*I wish to dedicate this book to my two sons, with whom I share my love, laughs and happiness with.*